THE
ROAD LESS TRAVELED

THE
ROAD LESS TRAVELED
FORGOTTEN HISTORIC HIGHWAYS
OF NEW ENGLAND

Jn grant,

with all good ists

Rt A. fir

R O B E R T   A .   G E A K E

AMERICA
THROUGH TIME®
ADDING COLOR TO AMERICAN HISTORY

In memory of Donald R. Charland, 1928–2016

America Through Time is an imprint of Fonthill Media LLC
www.through-time.com
office@through-time.com

Published by Arcadia Publishing by arrangement with Fonthill Media LLC
For all general information, please contact Arcadia Publishing:
Telephone: 843-853-2070
Fax: 843-853-0044
E-mail: sales@arcadiapublishing.com
For customer service and orders:
Toll-Free 1-888-313-2665

www.arcadiapublishing.com

First published 2019

Copyright © Robert A. Geake 2019

ISBN 978-1-63499-198-8

Typeset in 10pt on 13pt Sabon
Printed and bound in England

PREFACE

Throughout New England—between, among, and sometimes alongside the many freeways we have constructed to make our commutes to and from work more time efficient—we have those now lesser roadways that were constructed at the time of our young nation's first spurt of growth. Roadways and byways were once the arteries on which flowed goods of all kinds in ox-drawn wagons, carried individual riders on horseback, and passengers by stagecoach or upon open brakes. In the summer, travelers might ride an open curricle, and in the fall, the enclosed brougham with its driver outside and upfront on a seat behind the team of horses.

In the twenty-first century, with our all-consuming worry about time, it may be difficult to conjure those roads we traverse so casually and swiftly back to the times of plodding horses and swaying coaches. Yet there are still sections of old highways and turnpikes in the region that allow the traveler to imagine those days because they are seeing houses and farmlands, stonewalls, sites, and sought-after places of long-time memory that travelers nearly 200 years before had also seen.

This is a book I have wanted to write for some time, but more "serious" histories seemed to call to be written. Even then, as I wrote of early settlements and the history of New England's early development, I was drawn to finding stories of people who lived during those times, the life lived between the dates of birth and death, beyond the livelihood given them. As I have in earlier books, I hope to shed some light on those histories as we travel along what are now the backroads of our communities.

It is both intended to be a kind a travel guide and a reflection of the author's own experiences on the roads he has traveled—some for many years and others new to him—as he constructed this narrative.

CONTENTS

1

EARLY ROADS AND TURNPIKES

Long before the arrival of Europeans, indigenous footpaths crisscrossed the land that would come to be known as New England. Roads were but slowly improved from these paths, as early settlements began along the coast and the inland rivers that were so abundant in the area. Transport by water was the preferred route that shipped goods from town to town along the inland waterways and ferried the produce, livestock, bricks, and limestone to the larger coastal communities.

Initially throughout New England, proprietors, or landowners, were required to maintain roadways along their property. Areas outside of the boundaries were the responsibility of the town. This was not always an advantageous arrangement, for if the landowner was negligent in maintaining the roadway, travelers found the going slow. A Mr. Thurber traveling from Pomfret to Providence in 1776 found he had to keep the horse pulling his chaise "at a slow walk but little of the way."

Many communities came to see the need for uniformity, as they did in Pomfret, Connecticut. In March 1726, the proprietors "agreed to make over to the town all highways in the purchase. The town then went forward with the work of making roads and bridges as occasion and circumstances required."

The roads were maintained through laws adopted in many towns that mandated every able-bodied man in town was to commit to a few days' work on the roadways each year. As is usual in New England, the law only goes so far. The reluctance of many to perform hard labor led to hirelings, and these "half-hearted" laborers performed their task so poorly that bad roads were the bane of travel for a good century after many had been constructed.

Road construction in this early period was performed using oxen, with one driver urging a pair of oxen forward as he held the handle of a plow, while the other on the beam overlooked the machine that moved along the sides of the roadway, turning every 50 yards. The large boulders and stones, unearthed, would then be moved by laborers to the sides of the road and the loose dirt raked to the center. A second pair of oxen would then draw a leveling box, called a stone-drag, along the new road. According to historian Stewart Holbrook: "On the steep hills, a succession of ridges was left across the road to divert rainwater to the ditches and prevent the road from being washed away." The last step in the road's construction was to dump gravel in the boggy stretches, or create a culvert, when deemed necessary.

If a ledge of rock was an obstacle, the men drilled holes into the rock by hand with what local drills were available. As this was before the time of dynamite casings and fuses, an old method of "laying a train of powder" was used, in that after the hole was drilled and packed with powder, a long, hollow quill was inserted, and duly filled with the tamping placed around it, "carried the fire to the charge."

Muddy roads in low-lying areas were another concern. Historian Frederick J. Wood, who wrote the authoritative book on these roadways with *The Turnpikes of New England* in 1919, explained to the reader:

> When the pioneer road builders had occasion to cross a swampy piece of ground, they made a bed of tree trunks set transversely to the road and closely adjacent to each other. This form of road was called corduroy, and over it the vehicles went in a succession of bumps, painful to the traveler and destructive to the running gear.

Once sawmills made it possible to lay boards of uniform thickness, "plank roads" were constructed in these areas. The Plum Island Turnpike in Massachusetts was initially laid with planking, and the state of Vermont approved fourteen such roads to be constructed by turnpike companies between 1851 and 1853. Typically, on a well-traveled roadway, the planking would be in need of replacement every seven years.

To maintain the roads, gangs of laborers would be recruited in June after planting, when the roads were deeply rutted from travel in the winter and spring, and when they were typically in great need of repair.

The King's Highway, a roadway that was originally the Pequot Path, was improved significantly in 1703, but it was not until 1792—when Congress appropriated funds for an official postal route from Boston to New York— that the Post Road, as it came to be known, was maintained with any degree of regularity.

Another roadway, which came to be called the Plainfield Pike, originated as an indigenous path between Providence, Rhode Island, and Norwich,

Connecticut. This improved roadway was completed by 1714, but travelers long after complained of its rough condition.

Traveling through Vermont, in a carriage that crept along the hazardous route in the wilderness, Rev. Timothy Dwight from Yale could only marvel at the locals, who:

> Over roads, encumbered with rocks, mire, and the stumps and roots of trees … ride upon a full trot; and are apprehensive of no danger. Even the women of these settlements, and those of every age share largely in this spirit. The longest journies [sic.], in very difficult roads, they undertake with cheerfulness, and perform without anxiety. I have often met them on horseback; and been surprised to see them pass fearlessly over those dangers of the way, which my companions and myself watched with caution and solicitude.

The Revolutionary War brought a boon of road improvement to far-flung areas, as soldiers and suppliers both had to use the roadways. It was during this period when, of necessity, the trend began to change from coastal and river trade to the inland routes of travel.

By 1800, many towns had accessed a tax to pay laborers and maintain supplies based upon the assessed property value of owned land along the roadways. The tax was agreed upon by vote. Still, many towns paid that tax in labor, and the problem persisted even as road traffic was increasing. On one Saturday in the winter of 1803, the toll keeper on the road between Berkshire County, Massachusetts, and Hudson, New York, recorded more than 700 sleds and sleighs, many of them loaded with goods for the markets, traveling on the road that day.

The solution came with the granting of licenses to turnpike companies. Among the first was the turnpike built between Norwich and New London, Connecticut, which was financed by lottery in 1789.

Between 1796 and 1806, some 135 corporations were formed that would lay some 3,000 miles of roadway through New England. Operating under a charter, each turnpike company would construct and maintain a private toll road, charging a set of fees for each type of traveler. Gates were erected to collect the toll. Turnpikes ranged from 3 to 50 miles. Each one had its original name and charged similar rates, though they were not uniform by any means. One such old sign bearing the road's "Rates of Toll," reads:

For one Carriage or Sleigh	
Drawn by 4 horses	25c
If drawn by 2 horses	15c
If drawn by 1 horse	10c
For Every Score of Cattle	25c
For Every Score of Sheep	12c

For Every Score of Hogs	18c
Foe Every Cart or Wagon	18c
For Every Horse and Rider	6c
For Every Tied Horse	6c
For Every Person on Foot	2c
Persons going to Church	FREE

Of the New England states, New Hampshire constructed some twenty-five turnpikes between its first, which was incorporated in 1796, connecting Concord (the state capital) with the port city of Portsmouth, New Hampshire, to the Mount Washington Summit Road, whose charter was granted in 1853 for a turnpike from the Peabody River Valley that crossed the summit and ended at a point between Notch and Cherry Mountain.

The state also holds the distinction of having granted the last turnpike charter in the region, but it was for a road that would never be built. Approval had been given to the Mount Prospect Hotel Company in 1893, with the intended route to connect the towns of Lancaster and Whitfield, with a side road to the top of Mount Prospect where the private summer home of Secretary of War John Weeks had been constructed.

The charter granted was never acted upon, and the road that takes the traveler to the summit of Mount Prospect is still the road that was the entrance to Weeks' residence.

Throughout the eighteenth and nineteenth centuries, improvement in the repairs of the road also grew in regularity, as did methods for leveling and "Patching" worn areas. Initially, gravel and a rough mix of dirt was often thrown down into ruts or worn areas while a horse drawing a heavy barrel-like leveler would follow.

The tradition of bartering time on the road repair detail *in lieu* of paying certain taxes in a township continued well into the eighteenth century, when men convicted of debt with be sentenced to serve time on the crew.

The improvement of turnpikes was advantageous, of course, to those who built them, and for a time, those who lived along the route. This was, of course, a disadvantage to other roads. Whereas the turnpike corporation kept the road in good repair, those assigned to the old "by mile" maintenance system fell deeply into disrepair, if one could call the route an entire road.

At the height of stagecoach travel, numerous coaches traveled the roadways back and forth from specific destinations along routes whose path was highly competitive. A new road would attract business into sleepy town centers, and eager investors who built inns or taverns along the turnpike would increase that business as well as tax revenue.

Pomfret, Connecticut, being an isolated agricultural hamlet by the early eighteenth century amid an increased growth of mill industries, stubbornly resisted the slew of proposed turnpikes that would travel through its territory. In the end, industry had its way at considerable cost to the citizens. Historian Dan Partridge wrote:

> So great was the outlay caused by all these turnpikes and bridges that it was proposed to sell the newly constructed town house. Before accounts were settled another turnpike was demanded—a direct road from Providence to meet the Boston and Hartford Turnpike in Ashford.

The variety of vehicle on the turnpikes began with ox-drawn and horse-drawn wagons bringing goods out to sell and supplies back over the roadways in each direction. Travel by horse was still a popular option, and one-way shays, a type of carriage just a cut above a trotter's sulky, provided cheap transportation. If you owned your own vehicle, the cheapest mode of transport might be a "chair." A common vehicle on New England roadways during this period, historian Frederic J. Wood described it as "hung upon springs made of wood, generally with rude bow or standing tops of round iron, hung around with painted cloth curtains. The linings and cushions stuffed with 'swinging-tow,' sometimes with salt hay ..."

He observed that "there were many shops which had been established in colonial days where fine carriages were occasionally built and many imported vehicles repaired. But business languished for lack of customers. The hard times which followed the Revolution made simplicity a virtue, and the luxury of a carriage was not suited to the democratic habits which then prevailed."

As economic strength and wealth began to grow in the young republic, demand for all manner of traveling vehicles grew as, for the first time, we came to feel our vehicle of choice was a reflection of ourselves. The historian explains:

> The chaise was early in great demand, and down to 1840 it seemed that nothing could supplant it in popular favor. The earlier forms had enormously high wheels and the tops were stationary, being supported on iron posts.

Other vehicles on the road in the late eighteenth and early nineteenth century included the "curricle," adapted from an Italian design that set the box on leather braces. By the late eighteenth century, springs had been added, as well as a spring bar across the horses' backs. "It was a vehicle of easy draft and could be driven at great speed, but it was rather dangerous if the horse shied or stumbled."

These, along with coaches, landaus, phaetons, gigs, and wagons and carts all traveled the early roadways of New England.

One-way shay. (*Illustration from the author's collection*)

With the introduction of stagecoaches to transport passengers to and from destinations, both the style and comfort of the vehicles underwent major improvements. In the early part of the nineteenth century, the crude coaches used after the Revolution were replaced by an egg-shaped coach, the body hung high on leather braces above the axles of the four large wheels. There was a footboard and seat outside behind the horses and three seats inside. The boot for baggage was sunk behind the rear wheels and enclosed with curtains. An illustration of this style of coach was usually found on advertisements of the era.

Obidiah Elliot's invention of the elliptic spring in 1804 allowed coach manufacturers to reduce the size of the wheels and lower the body nearer to the road for easy entry and exiting of the vehicle.

Manufacturer Louis Downing of Concord, New Hampshire, first produced the popular "Concord Coach" in 1828. These coaches were the most reliable of transportation for the next ninety years, as Wood described in 1919, the Concord Coach "leapt into popularity ... on account of its excellence in workmanship and from its ease in riding." According to the historian:

> ... in the construction of our first railroad cars the builders could think of nothing better, and Concord Coach bodies, mounted on railway trucks, followed the first locomotive over the Mohawk and Hudson Valley in 1831.

As turnpike corporations subsided in the 1840s, towns or the state took over roadways, though many remained in poor repair until the W.P.A. projects of the 1930s rejuvenated many of the renumbered and improved roadways for automobile traffic.

Railroads moved the goods and commerce that had once been transported by wagons on the turnpikes. Passengers too found train travel an upgrade from the horse-drawn coaches, and towns clamored for passenger service as they had once sought to be in the path of the great roadways that linked the rural townships with the coastal cities, and from there, the world.

The end of an era of the great roadways had come. They would be "improved," diverted, broken up into parts of later routes, and finally overshadowed by the new expressways built beginning in the Eisenhower era and into the 1960s when Interstate 95 was constructed; running the length of New England through the mid-coast cities down to Florida. Other expressways crisscrossed the region, and commerce built along newer roadways left those old roads that had once been so important to the growth of a community in decline.

In revisiting these places, we find that the creation of public spaces, such as parks, and the preservation of historic communities have all succeeded in allowing us to still get a glimpse of this past and give us the opportunity to secure them for future generations.

2

WHAT IS IN A NAME?

Throughout southern New England, we find an assortment of oddly named roads connecting with the main routes with more practical names.

Those of us who live in the region have become accustomed to the indigenous place names that still exist and the roads that sometimes bear the names as well. In addition, those roadways are names after notable Native Americans associated with the area. Early English road names in New England were often simple and practical, denoting their use or destination.

Off West Main Road, for instance, in the town of Portsmouth, Rhode Island, lies Mail Coach Road. This exists from the period when the mail coach would use this lane as a turnaround to take the long road (now named Union Street to West Main Road). At the intersection of West Main Rd. (Rt. 138) and Union Street sits a former church, which now houses the Portsmouth Historical Society. The society maintains a small museum within the church, and also uses its space for talks and other events through the year. On the grounds there is also a nineteenth-century schoolhouse, and of particular interest to me, a barn in which lies an early nineteenth-century wooden box carriage for postal delivery.

In the town of Simsbury, Connecticut, amid the first settlement houses there, lies Hopmeadow Lane, likely associated with the brewing for the tavern on the road operated by Capt. Joseph Phelps by 1771.

As the main routes were improved, these long used practical names grew in usage, many routes simply named for their destinations such as the Hartford Pike or the Durham Road. Other early names, like Church Street, Grist Mill Road, Saw Mill Road, and Asylum Lane, spelled clearly what lies on their path. Farewell Avenue in Newport, Rhode Island, leads the traveler to the

Early twentieth-century post carriage in the collection of the Portsmouth Historical Society.

colonial cemetery. In other cases, however, the names are more mysterious to the visitor.

Not far from the Portsmouth Historical Society is Stub Toe Lane, a road that connects West Main Road with Middle Road. Other Stub Toe Lanes lie in Milford (near the Peppercorn Hill Conservation Area) and Southborough, Massachusetts, off Middle Road just before the Sudbury Reservoir. We can only assume these might have been named as testament to the consequences of trying to make it home on a moonless night along the rock-strewn dirt roads before lighting or pavement came to be constructed on rural roadways.

In Middletown, Rhode Island, visitors at the stop sign near Second Beach may be startled to find themselves at the crossroads of Purgatory Road and Paradise Avenue. Though some might seek religious meaning in the naming of these roads, the simple explanation is that one road leads past Purgatory Chasm, a natural rock formation with a deep chasm into which the ocean water crashes dramatically at high tide. The other leads into what was once called the Paradise Hills, and runs adjacent to Paradise Brook, and in sight of the ridge called Paradise Rocks that leads to Hangman's Rock overlooking Second Beach.

Paradise Avenue also leads to a modest, one-room schoolhouse built in 1875 and operated as the Paradise School for local children until 1955. It was used briefly for an administrative building and then purchased by the Middletown Historical Society, which continues to maintain the building and use it for meetings and events today. I had the privilege of giving a talk there a few years ago to a generous audience.

The popular "Concord" type stagecoach of the nineteenth century. (*Postcard from the author's collection*)

Adjacent to the historic schoolhouse is Paradise Park, a pleasant walking place that holds an eighteenth-century windmill within its grounds. Recently expanded trails also lead into the marsh beyond the site.

In Canterbury, Connecticut, Devotion Road is connected to both Cemetery Road and Toleration Road, and in Pomfret, Connecticut, Needles Eye Road leads to the Baffin Island Conservation Area, truly a place where one can commune with nature.

Road names were also attributed to those who owned the property on which the road ran, but others came to be associated with people themselves of some notoriety who lived on the road itself.

Such was the case with two particular roads in Maine. Jackass Annie Road in Minot, Maine, was named for Mesannie Wilkins, described as "a woman who liked to wear pants and speak her mind." She was not regarded kindly by locals who gave her the moniker for her habit of riding her donkey to her job every day at a shoe store in Lewiston. When the last remaining member of her extended family died in 1954, and with a diagnosis of a life-threatening illness, Mesannie decided at the age of sixty-three to take a long-dreamed-of trip to California.

Not traveling by conventional means, she packed her mule and took a horse and her dog for the 7,000-mile journey. She returned to Maine after a successful trip and moved in with a close friend, Mina Titus Sawyer, in Westfield, Maine. It was during those years that she compiled the diary and photographs from her journey into a book entitled *The Last of the Saddle Tramps*. She died in 1980 at the age of eighty-eight.

Years later, she inspired a California woman to retrace her journey to Maine. The town turned out to welcome her when she reached Minot, as well as to celebrate the woman once known in the town as Jackass Annie.

In the town of Greenwood, Alcohol Mary Road was named for a woman who lived on the short thoroughfare near Route 219 and made and sold liquor during prohibition. To the Hertel family, however, long believed to be descendants of the woman, the road has been the source of frustration. In 2011, Arthur Hertel petitioned the selectmen of the town to change the name.

He claimed that while his family had lived on the road, and his grandmother had been named Mary, the woman for whom the road was really named was a neighbor, who, like the Hertels, was part of the Finnish community that had settled in Greenwood. He no longer lived in Greenwood, but still felt the sting of the name's insinuation and had tired of the phone calls asking him about "Alcohol Mary." At the selectmen's meeting, however, residents decried the effort to change the road's name. Such was the outcry that the selectmen chose to keep the name.

The origin of what is now incorrectly recorded as Riddle Road in Manchester, New Hampshire, is no puzzle to those who know about the town's history. The road and "Riddle Place" are named for John Riddell, one of the earliest settlers in the area around Amosreague Falls in 1773.

Some road names came with the increasing identification of Americans with their country. Early road names were often associated with traditional indigenous names used to describe the landscape or a natural destination. In the colonial period, as towns expanded, for every Chestnut, Maple, and Oak Streets laid out, there are Washington, Union, and Liberty Streets throughout New England.

What of other anomalies? Some seemed named in the aftermath of natural disasters. Burndt Swamp Road, which appears in several counties, would be one example. Another would be the oddly named Locust Street, which leads through old farmlands of Swansea, Massachusetts. Others echo human catastrophes such as Smallpox Trail in Richmond, Rhode Island, which led past the home of an eighteenth-century family who succumbed to the dreaded disease.

Some, as with Biscuit Hill Road, part of which runs through the George Parker Woodland in Coventry, Rhode Island, have a legend associated with the name. In this instance, the dirt pathway at the time of the Revolutionary War was named so after a wagon of bread and biscuits headed for an encampment of French troops at the Waterman Tavern overturned on the hill. But what of Bacon Hill in Granville, Massachusetts, and Pudding Hill in Canterbury, Connecticut?

Some road names seem to warn of impending disaster. As I have lived in northern Rhode Island for nearly forty years, I have long been familiar with Breakneck Hill Road in Lincoln with its long and curving descent to the intersection of Great Road. I think it would be anyone's assumption that the road was then named for the danger faced if one took the hill at great speed. It should come as no surprise then that there are Breakneck Hill Roads in Killingly and Dayville, Connecticut, as well as well as in Southborough, Massachusetts.

It may be of some comfort that Lovers Lane is also a popular name for hidden roadways throughout the region. We can find one of Brush Hill Road in Granville, Massachusetts, as well as in Beckett and Great Barrington, Massachusetts. One lies on the map in Norfolk, Connecticut, and perhaps the longest lies in Torrington, as a wooded country lane that runs adjacent to Lovers Lane brook, between Goshen Road and Allen Road, which is Connecticut Highway Rt. 4.

3

THE GREAT ROAD:

SAYLESVILLE TO UNION VILLAGE, RHODE ISLAND

The Great Road, as it was named, was originally constructed from Providence, Rhode Island, to Mendon, Massachusetts, and opened in 1683. As with many ancient routes, the original has now been broken up, diverted, or disappeared in several places. However, there are still a few sections that have been preserved to afford the traveler much of the houses and landscape that a fellow traveler a hundred or more years before would have seen.

In those early years of Rhode Island history, The Great Road was one of a handful of footpaths and rutted lanes connecting the growing villages along the Blackstone and Moshassuck Rivers. Our drive will revisit the communities of Saylesville, Limerock, Manville, and Union Village.

The entrance to the Great Road from Front Street in the village of Saylesville in Lincoln, Rhode Island, is a good example. Standing noticeably on the right is the "splendid mansion house" of Eleazor Arnold, with the chimney rising above the roof as you approach the massive three-story, timber-framed stone-ender from 1693. The entrance to parking is on the right, at an entrance to the Gateway Park.

Eleazor Arnold was the fifth and youngest son of Thomas Arnold, who had acquired a large portion of land "at the end of the world," as the town dwellers in Providence called the sparsely settled area at the edge of their northwestern boundary. Eleazor was given the land as part of his inheritance in 1685. At that time, only one other house was being constructed along what would become the Great Road. That was Valentine Whitman's House, and the two "mansion houses" are alike in almost every respect, both two-story stone-enders with large garrets that are widely viewed as an adaption of an English Tudor cottage, including the Elizabethan-style chimney with its

Eleazor Arnold House, Lincoln, Rhode Island, 1693. (*Courtesy of Historic New England. Photo by the author*)

pillistered stonework. Eleazor's house was populated with Eleanor, his wife, and ten children, one a grown daughter, whose husband may also have shared the household for a time. His was largely a self-sustaining farm of 75 acres, holding a pair of oxen, sheep, cattle, and a horse.

Arnold was an active citizen of Providence, serving on the Town Council from 1684–1686, and served as a deputy of the General Assembly eight times between the years 1686–1715. He also served as a justice of the peace from 1705–1709. In 1710, he obtained a tavern license from the town of Providence and operated a public house with his son for about twenty-five years. Little changed inside the house, but that across from the large fireplace in the Great Room they partitioned a narrow alt-room in which beds were placed for patrons who wished or had no choice but to stay overnight.

Among the cots, according to Arnold's inventory at the time of his death in 1715, was included a bed with a pouch of tobacco reserved for an indigenous man apparently well known to Arnold. An area of what is now Lincoln Woods held a group of caves around a small natural pond, and it was said to be a gathering place for the varied tribes who passed through the region. It is likely that the elder sought a good bed for the night after visiting a place of memory that he had been to many times before, and he had reached the age where a straw mattress was more welcoming than the cold ground.

The Arnold family continued to live in the house until the early twentieth century when it had passed through generations of Arnolds. After his grandson, Preserved Arnold, a mill-owner who added an ell to the rear of the house in 1812, little seems to have changed, as noted by Historic New England:

> These later generations altered the house to suit their needs and changing lifestyles. During much of the 19th century, the house was inhabited by women who had been widowed by Arnold men or unmarried Arnold daughters. The circumstances of the time meant that when women were heads of the house, those periods were difficult and not as prosperous as when Arnold men were wealthy landowners.

The house was obtained by the Society for the Preservation of New England Antiquities in 1918. Now known as Historic New England, they maintain the house and offer school programs and tours on a regular schedule.

As we continue along Great Road, we come to the early nineteenth-century manufacturing building now known as Moffet Mill. The two-story wooden structure, built with a waterwheel dipped into the passing Moshassuck River, was constructed in 1812 by mechanic and toolmaker George Olney. The mill was one of the earliest metal workshops in the area, complete with a metal lathe and drill press, and it provided parts for machines employed at Capt. Wilbur Kelley's mill at Old Ashton, as well as the nearby Butterfly Mill, and his own Threadworks that he had constructed at a pond in Quidnnisuck woods.

The mill was purchased by Arnold Moffet in 1850, who altered the mill for his own woodworking business. A sawmill was installed, and Moffet manufactured wagons and furniture, as well as wooden boxes for customers nearby. He made improvements to the mill, replacing the waterwheel with a water-drawn iron turbine. Moffet installed braiding machines on the second floor around the time of the Civil War, and those years saw the manufacture of laces for shoes and corsets become a mainstay of the mill's business.

By 1880, a gristmill was installed and became part of the business at Moffet's mill. The sawmill still provided boards and sawdust for nearby residents, but the mill closed at the turn of the twentieth century. For more than ninety years, it lies abandoned, a collection of nineteenth-century machinery silent inside. Through the efforts of the Friends of Hearthside and other concerned citizens, it was stabilized in 2000 and restored to be open to the public several times a year; it remains under their stewardship.

Gradually, the Arnold lands began to be sold. In 1810, Benjamin and George Smith acquired land on both sides of the Great Road. After Benjamin Smith's death in 1830, his portion of the lands were sold to Jeremiah Whipple,

Moffet Mill (1850), constructed by George Olney. (*Photo by the author*)

and the accumulated property grew to contain over 118 acres. In 1867, some of the same parcel was purchased by Benjamin Ellery Chase, who built a small cottage for his wife and he to reside, and they established a farm. The land was passed down to their son, Charles Thornton Chase, in 1885, and he married Alice Crawshaw shortly after. A decade later, he built the two-story farmhouse, known as the Chase Farmhouse today.

The handsome farmhouse has its front door facing away from the road, as was the custom, with a drive leading past the front of the house and to a barn and other outbuildings beyond. While owned by the town of Lincoln, and abutting Heritage Park and its buildings, it is a private residence.

During his ownership, Charles T. Chase made more improvements to the property, utilizing a horse-drawn plow initially to expand an already existing pond at the crest of a hill on the property. In the 1920s, he used a steam shovel to expand the pond even more. His son and grandson would finally come to finish the project with a bulldozer in the 1950s.

By 1921, Charles had passed the farm on to his son, Benjamin Ellery Chase, who assumed the responsibilities of the farm. That same year, Benjamin married Wilhemina Gladys Westcott. They would have three children to raise on the farm.

The dairy that Charles had created was by then highly successful. Between 1884 and 1895, New England saw resurgence in dairy farming due to the wave of technology that brought pasteurization and bottled milk to the consumer.

Those of us who take such drives to view some of the old, existing farms (some rejuvenated by the farm to plate movement) hold a deep measure of respect for the amount of work any farmer faces each day. At its height, the Chase Farm held sixty to 100 Holstein cattle that needed to be fed, watered, and milked twice a day. Other chores included digging irrigation ditches, plowing and fertilizing fields, growing and gathering corn for silage and the grist mill, tending to the other livestock, and mending any needed repairs to the house, outbuildings, or barn.

In 1925, lightning struck the Chase Farm barn, and the resultant fire destroyed the building and a number of horses. The cattle were spared, as they were out to pasture during the advent of the storm. As the barn was appreciably close to the Arnold House, we can be thankful that great structure was saved. But with the large barn gone, Benjamin had but the stone dairy house for an outbuilding.

Benjamin soon acquired the adjacent Mariposa Farm from his neighbor, Joseph Sayles. The farm, whose name comes from the Spanish word for "butterfly," was added, and the combined properties became the Chase-Butterfly Farm. In the coming decades, a large barn and outbuilding complex would be constructed upon the lands around Arnold House, all but dwarfing the seventeenth-century structure.

The farm enjoyed continued success, and it was among the first dairy farms to deliver milk to the surrounding neighborhoods. The farm's herd of Holsteins could reportedly produce up to 25 quarts per cow per day. Benjamin and his son, Ralph, would continue to run the dairy farm until the mid 1960s. When Benjamin died in 1979, his widow sold the house, barns, outbuildings, and property to the town of Lincoln.

Through diligence and the hard work of many people, the Gateway Park was created, and its rolling pastures and hillside are open for dog walkers and hikers alike. The park also contains the Hannaway Blacksmith Shop, which holds classes on the craft regularly, as well as the so-called Hot Potato Schoolhouse, which was moved on numerous occasions during its lifetime.

The elegant stone and wood façade of Hearthside House is just down Great Road, and its origins are just as compelling as any of the many stories that played out along the road's history.

Called "The House that Love Built," the Federal-style mansion built by Stephen Hopkins Smith in 1812 is but part of the story of his remarkable life. Smith was the son of George Smith, who purchased land from the Arnolds in 1810. Prior to obtaining that land, the family of eleven lived in a modest stone-ender directly across the street from the site where Stephen would build his mansion.

Stephen Hopkins Smith was an extraordinarily gifted young man who would study both engineering and botany, and practiced later in his life what

Chase Farmhouse (1895), built by farmer Charles T. Chace for his wife, Alice, after a decade of marriage. They would raise three children on the farm. (*Photo by the author*)

Hearthside House (1812). The house was built by Stephen Hopkins Smith as a gesture to spurn forward an unrequited love. It failed and Smith never lived in the house. (*Photo by the author*)

we would now call landscape architecture. He was educated in Providence and there fell in love with both learning and a young woman who relished her social life among the town's elite families.

Hopkin's family could claim deep roots in Providence. His grandmother was a granddaughter of John the Miller, one of five people who had originally founded Providence with Roger Williams, and town clerk at the time of King Philip's War when he literally tossed documents into the Providence River to save them from the fire consuming the town.

His grandmother, Ann Smith, had become the second wife of Stephen Hopkins in 1755, making him a stepson of the governor. But these ties could not make up for his poverty. During their courting, perhaps to dissuade his intentions, the young lady made it clear that she would have to live in a grand house were she to marry.

Stephen Hopkins Smith was a true romantic. He earned a modest salary working for merchant Joseph Carrington of Providence, so when he won $40,000 in a lottery in 1810, he saw his chance and began constructing a house that would more than meet her expectations. Smith's vision of the house incorporated the use of the local fieldstone long used for the stone-enders built upon the road, but now, rather than one Elizabethan chimney, a pair of slender brick chimneys were raised and the stone used for the façade and all four walls of the house.

The mansion Smith built is a two and a half-story structure that features a gable roof flowing upward in graceful ogee curves to a beaded cornice above the circular windows of the attic. As the museum's description describe:

> The windows are topped by granite lintels and tall wooden pillars hold the full-height front portico, reminiscent of Mount Vernon, the portico is topped by a dormer which repeats the curve of the roof and beaded cornice

A similar portico was constructed above the side entrance as well, while the front portico originally included a balustrade around the dormer that was lost in the 1938 hurricane.

When the grand house was completed, Smith brought his prospective bride by horse and buggy to view the new home, never letting on that he had built it himself expressly for her. The young lady was reportedly quite impressed with the house, but wondered aloud who would choose to live in such a splendid house in the wilderness.

Stephen Hopkins Smith never moved into the mansion he built. He moved into another modest cottage nearby and let his siblings have the house, where they and their descendants enjoyed living for some 200 years.

He threw himself into managing the mill he built at the same time as the house, constructed with the same faced of fieldstone whose design would cause it to be called the "Butterfly Mill." Smith would eventually take a prime role in the construction of the Blackstone Valley Canal and continued his botanical interests as well, experimenting with improving fertilizers and landscaping much of the 242 acres that would become known as "Lincoln Woods."

An entrance to the park off the Great Road leads through much of the design, as well as the descendants of trees and flowering bushes of exotic origins that Smith planted, as well as the natural descendants of the forest the indigenous people called Quinnesuck. As we near the turn to continue on Great Road, the impressive mill with the stone butterfly design that Smith built still stands today.

Turning right, just after a farm stand whose silos rise in the distance along the roadside, we pass a series of newer homes before catching a glimpse of a finely restored house of the Georgian period, with its central door and five-bay windows above. The road continues past newer housing, and bearing to the right at a three-way intersection, we climb a hill past the elementary school on the right, and on the left, newer housing whose street names of "Bear Creek " and "Sweet Meadow" evoke an imagined past, until we reach sight of the Nate Mowry Tavern.

The two-story house had a long post and rail-enclosed porch, as well as a barn, and Nathanial Mowry built a large stable between 1800 and 1810. The stable kept fresh horses for riders and stagecoach drivers along the Great Road, and it was said that Mowry took great pride in having a selection of fine liquors from around the world at his public house. Now known as the

The Nate Mowry tavern (1800) distinguished itself by having the widest variety of world-made liquors of any other house on the Great Road to Providence. (*Photo by the author*)

Ballard Farm, the property has been a horse farm now for decades; it once provided shelter and pasture for the racehorses that ran at Narragansett Park. The farm has been owned and run by the Filippe family since the 1970s. They restored the 1810 barn and continue to run a horse farm on the property.

I had the pleasure of meeting Paul Filippe some years ago when writing a book about the state's historic farms. He was kind enough to show me the post and beam construction of the old barn.

Another impressive barn and carriage house lie on the property next door to the farm. The large Victorian carriage house with cupola is attributed to Dean Nickerson, having been constructed sometime after 1870.

Across the Great Road from The Mowry Tavern lies a cluster of small houses, one eighteenth-century clapboarded structure that was used as a store and a nineteenth-century Clapboarded two-story house. As we reach the intersection of Simeon Sayles Road, we see the fine, elegant Greek Revival House built by the Whipple family in 1823. Whipple was the president of the Smithfield Lime Rock Bank, and his house features a classic Doric portico, with the front doorway framed by a transom and sidelights. The house made quite an impression in its day. Nathaniel Mowry would build a similar house just up Anna Sayles Road some seven years later.

Tucked away off the intersection of Great Road and Anna Sayles and Simeon Sayles Roads lies the Mount Moriah Lodge No. 8. Originally a one-room schoolhouse, the building was expanded in 1804 and covered in brick. The lodge allowed the school to continue using the first floor while it held its meetings upstairs.

Continuing on the Great Road, we climb the curving hill of the road and take a right, past a new development on the hillside, and continue to Whalen Rd. Taking a right, we find the impressive Valentine Whitman house, strikingly similar to and completed a year after Eleazor Arnold's house on the opposite end of the Great Road.

Valentine Whitman was a valued and prominent citizen of Providence. He had come to Newport at just twenty years of age in 1648, working there to help raise funds to bring his other four brothers and father to America. He married Mary Aldrich of Suffolk, Massachusetts, on October 6, 1652, and within two years, he had brought the remainder of his family from Burton-upon-Trent. The family name there was Wightman, but for some reason, Valentine changed the spelling of his surname once in America.

He came to be a fluid speaker of indigenous languages, which he seemed to learn quickly in his first years in America. Roger Williams, the founder of the colony, knew him as "Richard Smith's man," when the elder Smith traded with native and new Americans for the furs brought to the shore of Cocumscussoc, a gentle cove lying just south of Wickford Harbor. Whitman later served as an interpreter during legal proceedings both against Native Americans and

Valentine Whitman House (1692). Almost identical to the Arnold House on the opposite end of Great Road and completed the year before said house, it is likely the same carpenters and craftsman worked on their construction. (*Photo by the author*)

in their defense. He served as negotiator between land companies from Connecticut and Boston seeking treaties with the various tribes in the region in 1658, and two years later, he was witness to the treaty signed by the sachem Ninigret with Hartford, New Haven, Plymouth, and Massachusetts Bay colonies.

In 1656, he served as the surveyor of highways and as commissioner in the Rhode Island General Court of Commissioners, and at the age of fifty, he enlisted as a soldier for the colony in King Philip's War.

Whitman was also a landowner who owned parcels in Warwick and Kingston as well as the parcel he owned near Lime Rock. In 1688, his taxable estate included 6 acres for tillage, 4½ acres of meadow, 4 of pasture, and 60 acres of woodland, as well as eleven cows, two steers, six yearlings, two oxen, two horses, and a mare.

Valentine Whitman died in 1701, but his house would pass to his namesake and only son among his nine children. Valentine Whitman, Jr., would also be an active citizen and played a role in town leadership. The first official meeting of the newly named town of Smithfield was held in the house in 1730.

We continue on Great Road again to the intersection of Rt. 116, which was named the George Washington highway on its construction. Here, the Great Road was broken up irretrievably, and so for our own purposes of exploration, take a right on to Rt. 116 and continue to the intersection of Rt.

126, or Old River Road. Take a left and continue past Lincoln High School and the pleasant suburban homes built across from the manicured fairways and greens of the Kirkbrae Country Club.

You will notice at once the long stone barn in the distance that was once part of the Theinart Dairy Farm. Continuing on to the intersection of School Street at the western border of Albion, we continue straight, past the nineteenth-century house and barn of the Samuel Hill Farm. The Handy Pond Preserve lies on the left as you continue on Old River Road and is a quiet spot for fly-fishing.

Just ahead lies the village of Manville. The village was a place of industry from its founding. As early as 1703, it held an ironworks with a large furnace built along the Blackstone River.

By the late nineteenth century, the village was the site of a massive mill complex known as the Manville Company, and later the Manville-Jenckes Mill, which at its height employed some 3,000 workers. The complex had its beginnings in 1878 and would grow to become one of the largest mills of its kind

In 1934, labor disputes rocked the mill industry in the Blackstone Valley. Workers went on strike in nearly all the mills along the corridor, and for the most part were peaceful demonstrations until Labor Day of that year when a strike was called in Rhode Island.

The owners of the Manville-Jenckes Mill defied the picketing laborers and decided to bring in replacement workers. Thousands gathered to repel the effort, and when two replacement workers managed to break through the picket line, a riot ensued. The Rhode Island State Guard, which had been dispatched by the governor to keep order, attempted to corral the strikers

Old wooden mill in Manville (*c.* 1810). The early years of industry in town foresaw the great mill to come in the later nineteenth century. (*Photo by the author*)

toward the nearby Moshassuck Cemetery, and an article from the *Providence Journal* on September 12, 1934 depicts the pitched battle that took place:

> The most stubborn fighting occurred in the Moshassuck Cemetery. Here hoodlums hid behind tombstones and pelted the troops with large rocks and other missiles ... when the guardsmen with bayonets and rifles and clubs charged into the cemetery, a pitched battle began over the long dead, and charging feet tore up clods of earth from the graves ... they (the strikers) ran in all directions when the rifles spurted and real bullets began to fly ...

The mill was damaged by flood in 1955 and destroyed by fire a year later.

Today, as we drive past the old Vose Farmstead and the later nineteenth-century houses built along Old River Road, the quiet village holds little trace of the changes once brought by the industrial age. Local resident Roger Gladu managed to save some of the memorabilia associated with the mill. The son of a fire chief in Manville, and a village fireman himself for forty years, Gladu keeps a small museum in his home of the village's history. He lent hundreds of photographs from his collection for the making of a documentary entitled *Senechonet to Manville: A Journey Through Time*, produced in 2004 by filmmakers Carlo and Betty Mencucci.

Nineteenth-century barn on the Vose Homestead, Manville. (*Photo by the author*)

Bearing left as we continue on Old River Road, we come to the intersection of Rt. 146. Take a right at the intersection and, within a short drive, you will notice a classic roadside attraction from a bygone era. Once part of the old Louisquisset Turnpike, Rt. 146 was once a two-lane country road. Now "improved" to a four-lane highway, few of the roadside attractions that were once a feature of the turnpike remain.

One that still remains is the iconic "Milk Can" that lies on the roadside as we head toward Woonsocket. Constructed in 1925 or 1931, depending upon the source, the classic ice-cream stand was moved to its present location as the state constructed Rt. 99. Featuring a 32-foot-high milk can, the structure was used as an ice-cream stand with takeout windows and a surrounding group of picnic tables for customers. While its original owners have disappeared from the record books, we do know that the owner by 1947 was Charles Plante, who sold the stand to Joseph Mariani that same year. The new owner improved the kitchen and expanded the takeout menu to include hamburgers and fried clams.

Operating as a seasonal business, the Milk Can became a popular attraction. Joe Mariani, Jr., remembered that the years he worked at the stand in the decade between 1955 and 1965 were among the busiest seasons for the restaurant: "We'd stay open until business waned," he recalled, "Sometimes we'd be scooping ice-cream until 2 a.m., especially on hot nights when people couldn't sleep."

With the death of Joe Sr.'s wife in 1968, the iconic stand closed. Numerous efforts have occurred over the years to restore and reopen the classic roadside attraction. When the plans to improve Rt. 146 were made in 1978, the state of Rhode Island acquired the property through eminent domain. Historic preservationists then began the effort to protect the structure, ultimately getting approval from the National Register of Historic Places. The state attempted to auction off the building in 1986, and while bids were received, officials failed to follow guidelines that came with the building's historic designation, and the auction was declared null and void.

A second auction the following year was successful but resulted in little improvement to the structure. By 1988, the D'andrea and Surtel families owned the building and made plans to move the Milk Can 1 ½ miles up the road to property they owned near a family business. They laid a new foundation for the structure and made plans for the move. Such an effort required the cooperation and support of three government agencies, the Rhode Island Department of Transportation, the Historical Preservation Commission, and the Federal Highway Commission.

The move also required that a special "cradle" be constructed so that the Milk Can could be moved horizontally to its new location. Eastman Brothers Movers were contracted by the state, and in December 1988, the structure was successfully relocated to its present site.

In the following months, the family invested in renovating the property, including the digging of a 90-foot-deep well to provide water in the new location. When the state tested the new well, however, it found that the water was highly contaminated. Some possible solutions were put forward, including laying a water line from the nearby family business, but with the death of D'Andrea in a motorcycle accident in 2004, the family's efforts to refurbish the structure seem to have ended.

In March 2018, the local *Valley Breeze* newspaper reported that a microbrew company had expressed interest in utilizing the structure, but as of this date, this classic piece of Americana remains unused and abandoned.

Continue your drive along the highway and bear right for the exit to Rt. 146A and follow to the intersection of Park Avenue. Go through the light and continue on 146A to the intersection of Providence Street (Rt. 104). If you are hungry at this point, a visit to the Beef Barn located at the intersection is well worth the stop. Continue straight through the intersection and in a few moments you will notice Smithfield Society of Friends Meeting House.

The Quakers who built the meetinghouse were originally part of the Providence Meetings until 1719, when they constructed a small, 20-foot-

Friends Meetinghouse, North Smithfield, Rhode Island. (*Photo by the author*)

square meetinghouse on this site. The original house was enlarged with the addition of a 20- by 30-foot-long ell in 1745. In 1775, this ell was removed and replaced by a 32-foot-square addition.

The house of worship was remodeled again in 1859, with green shutters added to what had long been a modest, white-clapboard façade. It was around this time that the issue of slavery began to be debated within the Quaker community in Rhode Island. Some of the Friends from this meetinghouse became involved in the Underground Railroad, particularly a woman named Abbey Kelley, who reportedly helped to smuggle escaped slaves from the south into Providence, and from there through the northern part of the state to Worcester, Massachusetts, and eventually to Canada.

Disaster struck the Friends Meeting in 1881 when the meetinghouse was destroyed by fire. Historian Thomas Bicknell would write of the site:

> The meeting house that now stands on the original land ... was erected in 1881 immediately after fire had destroyed the old building. News of the disaster was conveyed to the congregation while assembled in Quarterly Meeting and steps were taken at once to rebuild and this was quickly effected. The fire occurred on the 12th of May and the meeting was reassembled in the new meeting house on the tenth of November ...

A visit today in the early twenty-first century reveals that much has remained the same since the new meetinghouse was constructed. Lying close to the road, an asphalt drive and small parking lot are the only concessions the property gives to our time.

An interesting feature of this meetinghouse and its grounds is the natural cemetery that lies in a shaded area just to the north. There, a set of stone steps lead down the adjacent hillside to a small cleared area where a bench and a few large monuments stand. But scattered throughout the area are a number of smaller gravestones, some barely noticeable in the accumulated leaf clutter and ground cover on the woodland floor.

As the Smithfield Friends website explains:

> ... the forested area directly north of the Meeting House is a natural cemetery. Roughly 300 Friends from the 18th and 19th century are buried in this land, although only 100 Friends requested a gravestone or marker. The area is not pesticided or mowed. A natural canopy of trees is allowed to grow over the cemetery.

The meetinghouse remains an active place of worship, with pastoral meetings held each Sunday.

A short drive along what is now Smithfield Road brings us past the intersection of Woonsocket Hill Road and Peleg Arnold's large tavern. The house's origins date to 1690, when it was constructed by Richard Arnold, one of the first settlers in what is now North Smithfield. The tavern remained in the family and was expanded to its present state around 1790 by Peleg Arnold.

A justice of the state's Supreme Court, and representative to the Continental Congress, Peleg Arnold's tavern became the center of military operations in the town of Woonsocket during the Revolutionary War. Musters were held on the large lawn adjacent to the house, and recruiters used the tavern to enlist new men throughout the conflict with Great Britain.

Just down the road, we enter Union Village, which was officially separated from Woonsocket around 1800. Prior to this period, there were few buildings beyond the tavern. As the route was improved and stagecoach travel increased, builder Walter Allen constructed a number of the dwellings still existent today.

He constructed his own handsome two and a half-story house in 1802, attaching the Georgian-style dwelling to a small house constructed a century earlier by Hazadiah Comstock. He added a handsome, bay-door carriage house behind the house. Allen also built the Seth Allen tavern, with its unusual half-arched windows and twin gables, as well as a second tavern across Smithfield Road that became known as the Aldrich House.

The Stephen Brownell House and its handsome carriage house was also constructed by Allen. The ambitious builder populated this section of Smithfield Road all in the space of a decade.

Continuing our drive, we leave Union Village behind and in a short time Great Road returns on the right, taking us past several old houses, one that was reputedly an inn, before changing to East Harkness Road, which ends near the Massachusetts border.

The Stephen Brownell House (*c.* 1812) constructed along with other dwellings in early Union Village. (*Photo by the author*)

4

THE CENTRAL TURNPIKE:

NORTHBRIDGE TO OXFORD, MASSACHUSETTS

The Central Turnpike of Massachusetts was constructed, as so many others were, to establish faster routes between towns as the textile industry grew along the Blackstone and other rivers. Much of this route returns to the Blackstone Valley National Corridor, whose banners you will notice periodically on the roadside. Our drive begins at the entrance to this section of the corridor where a large mill house and the impressive Landow Mill, whose central tower is topped by a cupola, comes into view as Rt. 122N meets Court Street in Northbridge.

The town is most prominently known as a mill town, and, indeed, the brick mill built by Paul Whitin in 1826 dominated what is now the downtown area. Whitin had come to Northbridge from Dedham, Massachusetts, after the Revolutionary War, and he soon began work as an apprentice at an iron forge owned by Paul Fletcher. Whitin would eventually marry Fletcher's daughter, and the two would go into business together, establishing the Whitin and Fletcher Cotton Mill in 1815. Paul Whitin would buy out Flethcher's interest in the business in 1826 and establish the firm of Paul Whitin and Sons. Paul Whitin, Jr., and John C. Whitin proved to be astute businessmen.

Their success allowed the family to expand the mill in 1830 and again in 1845, turning what had been a small enterprise with forty workers at the original Brick Mill into an industrial complex that employed 146 townspeople. As the mill expanded, John C. Whitin built a large estate on a hill overlooking the mill and the Blackstone River that powered the machines within.

The grounds of the estate are now a park, with a carriage house being a remnant of the grand home, and a pavilion constructed to resemble the frame of a teahouse that once stood on the site. The park is a well-shaded respite,

The mill in Northbridge begun by Paul Whitin, as seen from the hillside park where his estate once stood. (*Photo by the author*)

with a fine view of the town, and it contains informational placards about the history of the mill, the family, and the estate. It also prominently displays a sculptured First Responders memorial.

The town buildings built during the industrial age reflect the wealth and confidence the textile industry brought to the town. Indeed, the elegant wooden houses built along Hill Street as you drive away from the downtown area were all built from the wealth the industry brought to Northbridge.

Further along upper Hill Street, we find the charming remnants of the pre-industrial town as we enter Whitinsville. It was here that the meetinghouse stood until 1835, and where the church and schoolhouse were located; it was the center of town.

The old two-story school, now a Veteran's Lodge, the stone wall-enclosed "Old Cemetery," the white Baptist Church, and adjacent farmhouses along this stretch before the central turnpike still gives us a charming glimpse of the days of horse and carriage, but for the SUVs parked in the driveways.

A short distance ahead, as we climb a hill to a stop sign, we take a left onto Sutton Avenue, also known as the Central Turnpike. The turnpike was improved as a private road by investors Samuel Slater, John J. Clark, and Joseph Valentine. Slater is a familiar name to Rhode Islanders, like me. He is widely credited with bringing the Industrial Revolution to America, after

Cemetery in Whitinsville in the old town center. (*Photo by the author*)

cribbing plans from the mill he helped to manage in England, and receiving financial backing from Moses Brown, of the Providence merchant family.

His 1793 mill, constructed in Pawtucket, Rhode Island, along the Blackstone River, was the first water-powered cotton-spinning mill in North America, utilizing what was known as the Arkright system of spinning as developed by Richard Arkwright in England. Slater hired women and children for his factory, a novel idea that spread throughout the mills in the Blackstone Valley Corridor, and whose strategy for filling the demands of the mills became known as the "Rhode Island System."

By the time of the construction of the Central Turnpike, Slater was heavily invested with production all along the Blackstone River Valley. The turnpike originally began in the town of West Needham (now present-day Wellesley), and continued west to Dudley, Massachusetts, on the Connecticut border, and continued on into Middlesex County as the Center Turnpike.

The rights to build a turnpike were given to Slater's corporation by the Massachusetts General Assembly in 1824, but the highway was not completed until 1830. Then, having constructed the route just a few years before the advent of railway transport began, the turnpike saw revenue for less than six years before the investors ceded the length of the road in Middlesex County to the state. By 1839, the corporation that had built the Central Turnpike had folded. The Connecticut section of the turnpike, overseen by the state, continued until 1853. Today, the turnpike is a well-shaded drive in summer, and a glorious spectacle of vibrant colors at the height of autumn.

Leaving Northbridge behind, we continue west past preserved farmlands interspersed with suburban housing. The turnpike's proximity to Rt. 146 has increased the development along this section in the past decade or so, but much remains of the road's past.

Shortly after passing the access to Rt. 146, we reach Purgatory Road and the entrance to Purgatory Chasm State Reservation. The park encompasses part of the 25-mile-long, 70-foot-deep chasm created some 14,000 years ago when an ice glacier melt carved out the chasm through the granite bedrock. The 1.6-mile chasm trail is surrounded by boulder caves and shadowed by high precipices, some named, such as Lover's Leap and "The Devil's Pulpit," which rise some 70 feet above the trail. The park is a favorite for kids that love to clamber over the rocks and explore the caves. For those of us who are older now, there is also a nice ridge trail that circles down and meets a lower trail at the end of the chasm.

As we return to the Central Turnpike, a farm or old inn will appear down the road when least expected, and as we reach the intersection of the Central Turnpike and West Sutton Road, we enter the West Sutton Historical District and a cluster of eighteenth- and early nineteenth-century buildings.

Two large, adjacent farms immediately appear to the left of the intersection. Across the street lies the old Samuel Waters Tavern (*c*. 1776).

The Samuel Waters Tavern (1776). Waters was raised in Sutton and was the village minister. His family owned Waters Farm, now a living recreation of an eighteenth-century farm. (*Photo by the author*)

It is believed that Waters constructed the house just north of the road leading to his brother's farm shortly after his marriage in 1776. The Reverend Samuel Waters served as the pastor of the First Baptist Church for twenty-five years. The church is just down the road at the intersection of Town Farm Road. Waters kept a tavern in his house, operated a distillery and ashery behind the house, and also operated two blacksmith shops—one that manufactured scythes for the local farmers and another for shoeing horses.

His son, Joshua Waters, constructed what became the main block of the house with its wooden arcade around 1802 and sold the house to his brother-in-law, Amos Waters. It was during this period that the great room on the second story of the house was used as a Mason Hall. A great mural is reportedly still intact on a wall of the second floor.

The young man who had married into the family would bring much hardship and shame upon the minister. Encouraged by his son-in-law to invest with interested parties in a cotton-manufacturing company, the family and stockholders of Sutton lost nearly everything.

Unable to pay his debts, Rev. Waters was arrested in 1817 and jailed in Worcester, Massachusetts. In this Hamiltonian era of banking and fiscal responsibility, many were arrested for debt. The majority of his fellow prisoners were victims of a creditor's insistence that time be served for a debt unpaid. Such prisoners waited helplessly until family and friends could pay the debt owed and secure their release. While there, Waters preached six sermons to inmates over the course of his internment; these sermons were later published with the preface that the sermons were "… within the walls of Worcester Jail, at the request of those, who, by confinement, lack the privilege of attending public worship, joined by other within the limits."

The majority of sermons seem to urge the men to accept responsibility for their own ill-advised actions, and not blame the money lenders that had placed them there but pray for them as well as their own souls. One sermon took its lesson from Matthew 5:8—"Blessed are the pure in heart, for they shall see God."

Just down Waters Rd. off the turnpike, we find the Waters Farm, now a preserved historical site and living history museum. The farmland is part of the 667 acres purchased by Richard Waters in the early 1700s. His grandson, Stephen, would build the main house in 1757. The farm currently holds 120 acres with the main house, a barn, and outbuildings on a hillside overlooking nearby Manchaug Pond. The farm is open for tours during summer and offers events year-round. Other great farms lie at the intersection of West Sutton Road.

Next door to the Samuel Waters Tavern is the Jonathan Dudley, Jr., House (*c.* 1826), a two-story, five-bay Georgian structure with a rear ell that features a central doorway highlighted by vertical transom windows on each side of the entrance.

One of two large farms that lie at the intersection of West Sutton Road on the turnpike. (*Photo by the author*)

Jonathan Dudley, Jr., (1738–1795) was a descendant of Samuel Dudley, one of the settlers of Sutton in 1714. He was the first son of Jonathan Dudley, who was born part of a set of triplets on November 1, 1709 with his brother, David, and sister, Abigail, a rarity for those times. In adulthood, Dudley, Sr., was a parishioner who was appointed to the committee that seated the new Baptist meetinghouse in 1760 and later served on a committee to raise soldiers for the Continental Army.

Dudley, Jr., built his house shortly after his marriage to Sarah R. Torrey. The house was later sold to Col. Reuben Waters who lived there for some years. It was later owned by James Phelps and then sold to carpenter Gardner Gibson. Numerous other families have owned the house since 1879.

Continuing on as we approach the town of Oxford, we reach the busy intersection of Lovett Road and the fine Georgian-style Campbell-Duncan House (*c.* 1757).

At the intersection of Rt. 12, you will have reached Oxford and the Main Street Historic district. Take time to park and stroll past the array of late eighteenth- and early mid-nineteenth-century historic houses and buildings. Among the oldest are the Universalist Church (*c.* 1793) and the John Wetherell Store (*c.* 1817). Later buildings were heavily influenced by Greek Revival of the early to mid-nineteenth century.

The historic section of town runs from Huguenot Road south of the intersection with Central Turnpike to Front Street at the northern end of town. Oxford offers multiple choices to dine during your visit, including the Slice of Heaven restaurant, situated in a classic Victorian cottage where you can dine at tables on the lawn, surrounded by a white picket fence.

Building on Main Street, Oxford, Massachusetts. (*Photo by the author*)

If a picnic is more to your liking, drive down to Huguenot Road and Fort Hill Road, which will bring you to the site of the Huguenot Fort. The Town of Oxford was originally settled by French Huguenots in 1687. The settlement laid out was part of Nipmuc Country, and indigenous relations were tenuous and turned hostile around 1693 with the attack on Brookfield, Massachusetts, that summer. The following summer, hostilities reached Oxford when a young daughter of the Alard family was murdered and two others kidnapped and taken to Quebec. That summer was particularly difficult for the settlers, one recording:

> … whereas the Indians have appeared several times this summer, we were forced to garrison ourselves for three months together, and several families fled, so that our summer harvest of hay and corn hath gone to ruin by the beasts and cattle which hath brought us so low that we have not enough to supply our own necessities, many other families abandoning likewise so that we have none left but Mr. Bondet our minister, and the poorest of the plantation.

One of those poorest members were the Johnson family, and in 1696, they were to suffer a similar fate as the Alard's a few years before. Daniel Johnson's modest house stood on the southern border of the settlement near the indigenous path later called the Woodstock Trail. Sometime after Johnson had left his house on August 25, a band of indigenous warriors entered the house and killed three children. Johnson's wife fled with the aid of a cousin, but on his return home, the unwitting settler was "met by the assassins and shared the fate of his children."

There is a rough stone memorial to the "Johnson Massacre" on the site of Johnson's home off Main Street. This second violent incident caused the departure of the remaining settlers. According to tradition, they held a final service in the church they had built, visited the small cemetery where those who had died were interred, and then gathered their belongings and took to the "rough forest road" that led to Boston.

Driving south along Main Street, a left onto Huguenot Road carries the narrow road immediately under a railway trestle, and then through forested hillsides to Fort Hill Road, which takes us to the site of the Huguenot Fort.

The fort had been constructed in 1694 after the violence visited upon the Alard family. The once impressive structure was described in George Daniel's 1892 history of the town:

> The Main block-house was thirty feet long and eighteen feet wide, with a double-walled cellar twenty-four feet long by twelve feet wide and six feet deep. The inner walls supported the floor beams; the outer wall three feet from this was made of heavy boulders, on a foundation about three feet deep and supported the logs forming the wall of the house...

The site today is a pleasant park of 8½ acres with a nineteenth-century memorial and sheltered placard that holds information about the fort that existed there, as well as a photograph of a scaled-down model, which is housed in the town's public library. The park is a fine, shaded place for a picnic before returning to the road.

OFF-ROUTE

Another worthwhile visit nearby is Bartlett's Bridge, a stone-arched bridge constructed across the French River in North Oxford.

The bridge was constructed in 1889 and designed by Worcester engineer Charles A. Allen at the request of mill owner Edwin Bartlett to replace an earlier wooden span. The handsome rough-cut granite bridge is 30 feet long with an elliptical span of 13 feet above the river, as part of Clara Barton Road.

The courageous Civil War nurse and founder of today's American Red Cross was born in Oxford on Christmas Day 1821. The modest house where she was born, and a museum dedicated to her lifelong commitment to veterans, is located on adjacent Ennis Road.

A cross, erected at the site of the Huguenot Fort, Oxford, Massachusetts. (*Photo by the author*)

5

THE NORWICH—WOODSTOCK TURNPIKE:

NORWICH TO WOODSTOCK, CONNECTICUT

The pleasant drive that designates much of this old route as a "scenic highway" has a long and often contentious history among the towns and villages it connects through Connecticut and over the Massachusetts line.

While the town of Putnam had early on lobbied for a road going from their town—then running through Pomfret, and on to Norwich and New Haven—proponents failed to secure financial commitments to develop a route. Pomfret had laid out routes to Windham Village and Ashford by the late eighteenth century but resisted further efforts to develop routes through the town. Taxpayers feared the heavy outlay and prospective imposts caused by such a project.

When a proposed road from "Hartford towards Boston to the Massachusetts or Rhode Island line" was submitted, town officials delayed the project again and again by moving the process as slowly as possible through committees, public hearings, and refusing to raise funds for surveyors. Despite these efforts, the Boston and Hartford Turnpike was completed, and the town had to levy a tax of three and a half cents on each citizen.

Finally, in 1801, the town accepted a proposed road from Norwich that would pass through the town and reach the Massachusetts line, even though the town again was forced to raise money to pay for the assessments made by the state committee for the road. The route was already, as one early historian noted, "a public thoroughfare from time immemorial…it is not known when this road was laid out, but it was improved from time to time and made more passable." The Norwich–Woodstock Turnpike Association was soon formed, and improvements along the road began.

Driving along the road's peaceful and often serene views, it is difficult to imagine those busy days of horse and stagecoach travel. You catch glimpses of what places were like as you reach the old town centers or see a farmhouse in the distance from what seems to be miles of fields from the roadside.

The original toll road left Norwich along the already existing Canterbury Turnpike, crossed the Shetucket River and climbed Kinsman Hill Road in Lisbon, and then on to Putnam, Pomfret, and Woodstock. The Turnpike Corporation dissolved in 1846, and thereafter, the route was designated throughout Connecticut as the General Israel Putnam Highway, State Highway 169. In 1932, however, much of the route was renumbered as State Highway 93. This designation lasted until January 1959 when the old route number was returned with the impending completion of Interstate 93. In April 1991, the Connecticut Department of Transportation designated the route an "American Scenic Byway."

Begin your exploration in Norwich itself at the old village center on East Town Street. Here, the classical homes of early settlers and the shops of artisans and craftsman remain preserved around a fine New England village green. A placard on the street side of the green identifies the houses and shops for the visitor, with a map of "Historic Norwich Green 1775–1783" taken from the wonderful book by Joan Nasie of the town during the Revolutionary War years. In wandering along East Town Street, I soon met a few gentlemen who were eager to share the history of the buildings.

The Norwich Historical Society is located directly across from the placard on the green, a classic gambrel-roofed brick schoolhouse from the early eighteenth century, graced by a cupola.

The nineteenth-century schoolhouse that now houses the Norwich Historical Society. (*Photo by the author*)

Next door stands a small wooden gambrel-roofed house that was the silversmith shop of John Carpenter. It has the distinction of being the only remaining wooden silversmith shop from that era. A rare example of one that did not succumb to fire as did so many other early smith shops.

Being the starting point of the turnpike, Norwich had numerous taverns, a handful of them around the green. The Peck Tavern (*c.* 1698–1717) was originally operated by Sarah Kemble Knight, who was to become a noted traveler and diarist, penning an indispensable portrait of the roadways and people met upon her travels in early eighteenth-century New England. The original tavern was enlarged in 1734 and, by 1754, had been purchased by Joseph Peck who died in 1776. The handsome Federal-style house beside the tavern on the Elm Avenue side of the Green was the home of Joseph Peck's widow, Elizabeth Peck. John Wheatley had purchased the tavern from Peck and continued to operate it throughout the Revolution. After his death, his brother, Andrew, sold the tavern to settle John Wheatley's affairs. A tree that stood at the corner of her house and before the tavern was the village "liberty tree" leading up to the Revolutionary War. The large Georgian-style tavern was thus the meeting place of local patriots.

The house was described by Mary Elizabeth Perkins in her *Old Houses in the Ancient Town of Norwich* as follows:

> This Inn was one of three celebrated taverns on the Green, and some old people still remember the large, old elm which stood in front of the house, among the boughs of which was built a platform or arbor approached by a wooden walk from one of the upper windows. From this high station, the orators held forth on public occasions…

The Peck house and tavern are just beyond the large Georgian house of Capt. James Carew.

Mrs. Peck's tavern lies within walking distance of the Lord Tavern closer to the courthouse at the top of the green. Built by Eleazor Lord, Jr., around 1760, the house was also dubbed the "Compass house" by locals as its front door faced due north. Its proximity to the courthouse made it a popular gathering place for lawyers waiting to have their cases heard. Little was changed of the house but for a portico entryway constructed in the nineteenth century. The tavern faced demolition in 1972 but became the first historic house purchased by the newly formed Connecticut Trust for Historic Preservation in 1976.

Along the East Town Street side of the green, the house that became the elegant home of Moses Pierce, and later a long-standing orphanage, had its origins as the Jesse Brown Tavern (*c.* 1790).

The house that Brown built was licensed as a tavern and became a main stagecoach stop in Norwich. Its reputation was such that President John

The Peck Tavern (center) held an enormous tree on its lawn that would eventually be attached by platform to the tavern itself. (*Photo by the author*)

Adams and wife, Abigail, visited on August 1, 1797. By 1814, the tavern had been purchased by William Williams, of New London, Connecticut, and a few years later sold to Capt. Bela Peck, the son of John and Elizabeth Peck. He was prominent in the Connecticut militia and operated the tavern until his death at ninety-two years old in 1850.

Moses Pierce purchased the house five years later and refashioned the house in the gingerbread style that was popular in the Victorian era. He would donate the house to the United Workers of Norwich to be used as a home for poor and orphaned children. The building was then named the Rock Nook Home, and the construction of wings on either side of the historic house allowed for a maternity suite and a dormitory to be added to the already substantially modified structure. Today, it houses offices of the United Community and Family Services.

The village meetinghouse in the form of the First Congregational church sits at the upper end of East Town Street, an early nineteenth-century wooden clapboarded structure with a Roman numeral clock on its belfry.

The present church was constructed in 1801, and it is the fourth meetinghouse to be constructed for the village. The first had been built around 1660 on the southeast corner of the green. The second was constructed upon the summit of a rocky prominence behind the present church that came to be called the "meetinghouse rocks." The church served as a lookout during King Philip's War.

A third meetinghouse was constructed in 1770 on the site of the first meetinghouse but was razed in early 1801 by a fire of suspicious origin. The congregation laid the cornerstone for the present church on June 18, 1801.

What began as a humble tavern constructed by Jesse Brown became the elegant home of Moses Pierce, and then, later, an orphanage. (*Photo by the author*)

The First Congregation Church (1801) is actually the fourth structure built on or near this site; above on a ledge are the "meeting-house rocks." (*Photo by the author*)

The building was extensively renovated in 1845 to reflect the Greek Revival style in the cornice and trim. A Roman numeral clock was also added to the tower. Of interesting note is that the original church organ in this building was once powered by water.

Behind the church is a stone staircase to the summit of Meetinghouse Rocks. The old stone stairway is steep, but it is supported by cable and rails along the way. Those older travelers may find a dirt pathway that leads to the summit located behind the town well that sits on a small lawn between the church and its neighboring building, a Greek Revival structure with an arched entryway and windows named Speerli Hall, constructed by the church in 1859. The summit is still used as an outdoor chapel today.

Leaving Norwich Green from East Town Street, return to Town Street at the southern end of the green and take a left on to Town Street, you will soon see the sign for Rt. 169, but before turning on to Washington Street, continue on Town Street and look right for the parking for the historic Leffingwell House.

This handsome colonial structure had its beginnings as a plain, two-room house built by Stephen Backus in 1675. It was purchased by Thomas Leffingwell in 1701 who requested, and was granted, license to keep a "public house for the entertainment of strangers." Additions were added to the house

The Leffingwell House (1675, 1701) opened as a public house in 1701 and remained an inn for three generations. (*Photo by the author*)

by Thomas, and later by Christopher Leffingwell, as the house was used as an inn by three generations of the family. Christopher was a valued provider of provisions for the soldiers of the Revolutionary War.

The Leffingwell House Museum is maintained today by the Society of the Founders of Norwich open on Saturdays from April to November.

To continue our road trip, cross Town Street on to Rt. 169 where we follow the old Canterbury Turnpike into Taftville, a nineteenth-century mill town. The route bears right on to Merchants Avenue and travels through a blighted neighborhood through to the Taftville–Occum Road, and the massive buildings of the Ponaham Mills. The textile manufacturing company constructed its first mill in 1871 with a second mill added to the compound in 1884. An office building was added as well in 1929, and the mill continued in business until its closure in 1970.

Today, the mills are being repurposed into luxury apartments, and the office building currently houses a furniture warehouse. Take another right and follow until the bridge at Newent Road, which crosses the Shetucket River. Bear left at the entrance of the bridge to follow Rt. 169. In short order, the road becomes the South Burnham Highway. Follow this to the Town of Lisbon.

As soon as one crosses the bridge the drabness of Taftville is lifted, and like the sun bursting through the clouds, the appearance of green farmlands and outbuildings come into view, and almost immediately you are in Bliss.

That literally is the name of this area of Lisbon. The road quickly becomes a country lane, or what one Connecticut journalist and Beatles fan dubbed "the long and winding road."

A landscape of suburban-style houses alternating with woodlands takes up much of the drive. An occasional farm will appear, and remnants of stonewalls that once separated miles of pasture and fields now crop up now and then for long stretches beside the road, but these are often overgrown with briars or shrubbery.

Before long, a classic white Federal-style house appears ahead on the left; on the right is a white church, with another great house at the intersection ahead.

The house is the John Bishop House (1810), built by a descendant of one of the first families to settle in the Newent section of Lisbon when it was still a part of Norwich. The Lisbon Historical Society today runs the house as a museum. The house contains eleven rooms and is noted for both the well shaft located in the buttery and the seven fireplaces that are located throughout the house. Hearth cooking classes are regularly offered at the museum along with other events.

Across the street lies an impressive stonewall, part of the lands adjacent to the Newent Congregational Church.

A farm in Bliss, just over the bridge from Taftville. (*Photo by the author*)

The John Bishop House (1810) is now a house museum in Lisbon. (*Photo by the author*)

Continuing along Rt. 169, we soon see another historic house that the historical society has had a hand in restoring for the past four to five years. The Burnham Tavern (1755) was the site of gatherings during the Revolutionary War and a focal point for townspeople to get news of far flung battles.

The structure had long been in decline when the Town of Lisbon purchased the house from the last remaining family members in 2012. Two years later, the tavern was declared a state historic site, and the Lisbon Historical Society signed a ninety-nine-year lease on the 5-acre property.

A state grant of $50,000 allowed the historical society to make emergency structural repairs to the foundation and the rotting sills, which had allowed much structural damage to occur.

In the course of reconstruction, a number of interesting artifacts were found: pieces of plate, glass, metal, and part of an early brass spoon. A side door to the house, which had been covered for years, was exposed as well, though generally, as Ken Maher of the society's building committee told the press, the house had seen few renovations over the years, as it had passed through so few families.

The Burnham Tavern will hopefully soon be open to the public for tours beyond the occasional events held the past few years.

Continuing along Rt. 169N we soon enter the outskirts of the Town of Canterbury. Once part of Plainfield, the populace declared its independence in 1703 and became like its neighboring towns, long-standing agricultural farms

The Burnham Tavern (1755) is now under renovation by the Lisbon Historical Society. (*Photo by the author*)

and fast-growing mills along the Quinebaug River, which were the town's thriving industries.

Maintaining a reliable bridge across the river soon became one of the primary concerns of the town. The first bridge built by "two gentlemen of Plainfield" in 1728 was soon swept away by flood. Samuel Butts of the town replaced this bridge in 1733 and managed to maintain it with the help of subscriptions before it was destroyed by an ice floe.

Jabez Fitch built a bridge at another location, and by 1740, he had obtained permission from the General Assembly to charge a toll, as his was "the only one south of Sabin's (bridge) in Pomfret." His bridge was severely damaged in a flash flood of 1757 and rebuilt three years later.

Mill operators were granted permission to build dams along the numerous waterways "on condition of erecting a good cart bridge over it," though the dam that Ezra Ensworth requested to build along the river in the southern part of town to support his corn mill in 1761 was reluctantly granted, as any change "in the way of the annual ascent of the shad up the river was most vigorously resisted by all the residents in the Quinebaug Valley."

When this dam and Butt's bridge below were destroyed by ice jams in the winters that followed, the townspeople refused to rebuild the bridge or the dam. By then, the town held an agreement with neighboring Plainfield in helping to maintain the bridge on the "great public thoroughfare" (Rt. 14), as well as a fjord near Shepherds Hill in the northern end of town. The populace also helped to keep up bridges over Little River and Rowland's brook.

The cost became so great that the town was forced to petition the General Assembly for aid in 1782 as "they were obliged to maintain a large number of bridges in said town, many of them across large and rapid streams." These included "one and half of another over the Quinebaug, four over Little river, and six over Rowland brook."

It should come as little surprise then that citizens of Canterbury opposed construction of the proposed turnpikes through town, aside from the "great road" that led from Plainfield to Windham. When the state made the road a turnpike in 1799, the town so disparaged the gate erected near the center of town that it was removed in 1804, and gates were constructed near each end of the turnpike.

The town raised a committee to enlist the aid of other towns in opposing the proposed Norwich and Worcester turnpike in 1801, though their protest had little influence and the charter was granted to the company, which included tavern keeper Jedidiah Johnson of Canterbury.

An earlier tavern keeper would influence the route of the Norwich–Woodstock turnpike as it passed through the town. The original survey for the road was marked to run due north and south over the area known as Westminster Plain, but the owner of the old Park's tavern, located a half-mile east, induced the road's engineers, it is said, with the aid of spirituous liquors to route the highway past his tavern door.

Just south of Canterbury, keep an eye out for the impressive house of Capt. John Clark. The house was enlarged in 1800 to reflect the distinct "Canterbury Style" of the local builders, including the hip roof, Palladian window, and gable over two separate entrances framed by exquisitely crafted woodwork. You will notice similarities to the Prudence Crandall House Museum further down the road, which was also attributed to Clark's design.

As we reach the historic center of Canterbury, the First Congregational Church appears on the right. Slow down at the approach of the intersection with Rt. 14 and either park at the church or at the Crandall Museum (take a left on Rt. 14 and then another into the museum's parking lot to explore colonial Canterbury).

The present First Congregational Church was constructed in the 1960s, but it stands on the site of the first meetinghouse built in 1711. Across the street is the Col. Simon Lathrop House (*c.* 1746), which served as the church parsonage from 1842–1975. To the left of the old parsonage is the later Georgian John Carter house (1760), with an extended entryway topped by a triangular pediment.

Follow Library Road off the church green to find the Green District Schoolhouse (1850), a one-room schoolhouse that was used into the 1950s. It was later used as a library for many years and is now maintained by the town's historical society. Tours are advertised several times a year on the society's website.

Cross the street to the impressive house that sits on the intersection of Routes 169 and 14. The house was constructed by Elisha Payne in 1805 with the same attractive features of the Clark house, being the roof gable on hip with twin chimneys and the projecting pavilion of the two facades, with the impressive fluted pilasters that frame entryways and the Palladian window above.

In 1831, Prudence Crandall, a well-respected schoolteacher, was invited to move to Canterbury and open a school for young women of the town. The result was the formation of the Canterbury Female Boarding School in the Payne house, which Crandall purchased with a $500 down payment and a $,1500 mortgage.

The school was highly successful, bringing many of the well-to-do families' daughters of the town to its door, as well as earning a reputation that prompted neighboring towns and villages to enroll young women as well.

Just two years after this undertaking, a seemingly inauspicious event would bring to light deep-routed prejudices in the town and draw national attention to what had been a quiet, but prosperous New England community.

In 1832, a young black woman named Sarah Harris approached Prudence Crandall about receiving "a little more learning, if possible, to teach colored

The Green District Schoolhouse (1850) in Canterbury. (*Photo by the author*)

The Prudence Crandall Museum, Canterbury. (*Photo by the author*)

children." Miss Harris' request was accepted, and she was allowed to attend and live at the private school, working her way by doing chores and cleaning at the school to pay her tuition. It was not long before Miss Crandall received visits from irate parents who had sent their daughters to the school. The uproar over allowing a black student in the school infuriated Prudence Crandall, who dismissed all the white girls from the school and determined to turn her academy into the first school for African-American women in the county.

A public meeting was held in March 1833 and a delegation was formed to persuade Miss Crandall to abandon her plans for a school "for young ladies and little misses of color," but she stood firm in her purpose.

The remarkable story of Prudence Crandall's school, the black students who attended, and the ensuing turbulence and violence caused by citizens of the town are impressively presented at the present house museum.

Leaving Canterbury, continue on Rt. 169N for several miles to Brooklyn, easily noted by the large fair grounds you will pass on the left. Continue on to the old center of Brooklyn. The area was settled in the late seventeenth century and was a well-known indigenous gathering place along the Quinebaug River—the Brookline, or natural border, as described in the original deed.

Brooklyn became its own village in May 1786, and it is the final resting place of the Revolutionary War hero and Connecticut icon Israel Putnam.

A typical school desk of the period. Courtesy of the Crandall Museum. (*Photo by the author*)

Originally buried in an above-ground tomb at the South Burial Ground, visitation and vandalism soon forced the village to a more secure solution. In 1888, the village erected an equestrian monument just south of the green. As you enter the village, the statue stands on the left just past the brick post office and the Civil War monument.

The statue holds an erect Putnam on his mount, as though reviewing the troops, and the tiered concrete foundation, with its brass relief of oak leaves encircling just beneath the crown, holds the general's remains behind a granite slab engraved in his honor. The life of Israel Putnam has long fascinated me, from his young years famously tracking and killing a wolf responsible for wreaking havoc on the livestock of the town that would one day be named after him, to the portly, irresponsible, and somewhat mad Revolutionary War general who executed men seemingly at will, including a sixteen-year-old boy at a place that came to be known as Gallows Hill.

The barn-like fire station on the right and an old inn repurposed as a bank lead you past the domineering, seven-story tower of the Congregational Church into the heart of Brooklyn and its intersection with the old Providence–Hartford Pike, now U.S. Rt. 6, another well-traveled road for generations before it was improved as a toll road in 1826.

Brooklyn Town Hall, at the junctions of the Norwich–Woodstock turnpike and the old Hartford Pike.

The Brooklyn Town Hall sits on the corner of the intersection, and surrounding it on either side are nineteenth-century buildings that served travelers of the day in a variety of forms. Continue on Rt. 169 straight past an old store of this type, now largely abandoned but for use as a karate studio.

Just past the intersection, a junk lot and an old portico of a gas station appear on the left with the hand-painted DIESEL sign telling of well-traveled days in the not too distant past. Drive on past houses old and modern, with finely manicured lawns interspersed with undeveloped fields and woodlands. An old white colonial house appears on the left, with its smattering of outbuildings and barns. As with other old houses whose ends faced the turnpike, a side door was created at the end of the house and steps dug into the hillside, while its main entrance on the dirt drive is shaded from view by a fruit tree planted as they often were off the corner of the house.

Continuing ahead, other old turnpikes intersect with the Norwich–Woodstock route, Routes 101 and 44, traveling east–west, were all stagecoach and toll roads that crisscrossed the region. Routes 169 and 44 merges at this juncture. Just past the intersection of Route 101, look for signs for the Audubon Society's Bafflin Sanctuary. This beautiful conservation area contains the property from two adjacent farms, and the 2½-mile loop trail provides sweeping vistas of meadows, interspersed by wooded copses and stonewalls. It is a place that my family and I have visited numerous times over the years, especially in the fall when the colors of the wooded hillsides are at, or near, their peak. One ancient maple grown beside an equally ancient stonewall has been a landmark of ours for years, and coming back to the sanctuary through the decades and looking for that old maple has come to seem like visiting an old friend.

Continue your drive on Rt. 169N and you soon enter the old center of the town of Pomfret. Land for the town was purchased from Native Americans as part of the "Mashamoquet Purchase" in 1686. The town was originally named for the West Yorkshire village of Pontefract, and it was incorporated in 1713.

The town green was established on Pomfret Hill, just above Needles Eye Road; for many years, the First Congregational Church stood on the eastern edge of the green until destroyed by fire in December 2013. The Pomfret School, a well-known college preparatory school, was constructed across from the church in 1894 and remains today. Across the turnpike, an elegant house set back from the roadside was the Ben Grosvenor Inn, a highly popular resort hotel of its time during the late nineteenth century.

As you head towards the intersection, you will notice a large late colonial house. This is the Ann Hall house (1780), which was moved on to the property in 1934 from its original site. Ann Hall was a successful painter of miniatures in the social circles of early nineteenth-century New York, known particularly for her depictions of children and bridal portraits. She was born in the house in 1792 and showed considerable talent as a child. She and her sister, also a talented artist, were sent to her mother's family home in Newport to study with Samuel King, an earlier teacher of Gilbert Stuart. Both sisters later lived under the same house in New York City where Ann kept a studio on the top floor. Wealthy clients paid her as much as $500 per commission. She never married and died in her sister's home at the age seventy-one.

As you reach the present green and the convergence of the Norwich–Woodstock (Rt. 169), the Providence–Putnam Pike (Rt. 44), and Deerfield Rd. (Rt. 97), there is much that remains along the intersections from the period when stagecoach traffic and travelers on horseback cantered by the common.

This area contains the Pomfret Street Historical district, and includes houses, businesses, and barns dating back to the colonial period, as well as the large, elegant summer "cottages" built and set back on sweeping lawns by wealthy urbanites who made the village a summer resort in the late nineteenth and early twentieth century.

An old general store can be found just off the intersection on Deerfield Road (Rt. 97). This was the dwelling and general store of a merchant named George Washington (1732–1799). The precise date the house was built is unknown, listed only as "pre-revolution" in a survey of the town's historic houses during the W.P.A. years. The first floor was used as a general store until 1855 when it was converted into apartments. The survey also yielded another fact about the building: that a long-standing tale associated with the store was that Gen. Washington stopped by to purchase tobacco while traveling through Pomfret. The president did stop in the town on Saturday November 7, 1789 to inquire after the residence of Gen. Israel Putnam. Washington was on his way to Hartford, so the story may in fact be true. As it turns out, he continued the 8 miles on to Ashford Connecticut rather than travel to the home of Putnam. The story begs the question, however, whether it was the auspicious occasion of two George Washington's meeting one another at a general store in Pomfret.

A period barn still stands behind the house, and an out-building has long been converted into a restaurant-café called the Vanilla Bean Café. Further down the road, the old Carter Store also predates the Revolutionary War.

On the green is a stone monument, whose brass plaques bearing the names of the townsmen sacrificed in the Revolutionary and Civil Wars have darkened almost to the color of the stone; so too, as Pomfret progressed, did the townsmen's humble homes and businesses.

Several of the remaining colonials along this junction of the Providence–Putnam turnpike are associated with the Grosvenor family. At the eastern corner of the junction is the handsome Augustus Hoppins house (1800). Other colonial houses remain on side streets along the historic district.

The old general store and dwelling dates from pre-revolutionary days. (*Photo by the author*)

The Carter store, established in the same period on the Deerfield Road. (*Photo by the author*)

As you continue on Rt. 169N, a grouping of simpler farmhouses and barns appear. The road continues along the grade of a hill with wide fields on the left fenced in by a continuous wooden rail fence, while the hillside on the right is at first bordered by a stone wall and then a loosely connected line of trees, with the hillside open and gently sloping upward from the road.

Fox Hill Road intersects from the left, and soon another large farmhouse appears, with a secondary house across the lane at the intersection with Harrisville Road. Continue past fields and wooded copses for a time and then a large red barn complex takes up the hillside to the right, beyond which is the landing strip of the Woodstock Airport.

Continue past a grouping of houses and past the modern buildings of the Middle school and the Woodstock Academy. Founded in 1801, the expansive grounds and buildings of this independent high school provides education for residents from neighboring Brooklyn, Canterbury, Eastford, Pomfret, Union, and Woodstock. Tuition is paid by municipal taxes from the respective towns. The academy is widespread along this stretch of Rt. 169, with two more branches all the way to the northern branch in Woodstock.

The road merges for a brief time with Rt. 171, along which lies myriad repurposed structures, including Scranton's Antiques.

Scranton's Antiques, amid a grouping of houses and buildings along Rt. 171. (*Photo by the author*)

I have to admit that I spent years trolling through antique stores and buying odds and ends that were added to what is now a contented house cluttered with books, plants, music, and glassware shuttered in windowed cabinets, stoneware often topping those, or wedged between volumes on a bookshelf.

Tucked in the midst of all this are the little treasures I have found over the years, even if it is but a smooth stone from a faraway beach. Glass bottles on a windowsill, pictures and wooden signs on the wall, books from a lifetime of browsing, and, indeed, the chair in which I sit as I write at my desk are all testament to my weakness for antique stores, yard sales, and roadside stands.

Continuing on Rt. 169N, the merge with Rt. 171 quickly ends the intersection on "Bald Hill," with Rt. 171 bearing left past a dilapidated old store, and Rt. 169N continuing straight past a grouping of modern, suburban-type houses; when you bear left at the fire station, you have entered the Town of Woodstock. Drive on past the town hall and selectmen's office, and along the divided fields of a large estate, the large two-storied colonial now known as the Inn at Woodstock.

As you continue, look for a grand old double-chimney colonial house on the left side of the road. Take note, as a second, near identical house lies further down the road. Yet another similarly designed house, plainer and without

Roseland Cottage (1846), Woodstock. Courtesy of Historic New England. (*Photo by the author*)

shutters, appears again on the left. It may be that these were early nineteenth-century mill houses, prettied up except for this last, in the past century.

The First Congregational Church appears on the right, and then the stone monument that flanks the end of the green and the intersection with Roxbury Road. Bear left to follow Rt. 169N and drive slow as to be sure not to miss one of the most unique houses in New England.

The "pink house," as it has come to be known, has been one of the most iconic buildings in Woodstock since it was built as a Gothic Revival summer cottage in 1846 for wealthy New Yorker Henry Bowen. Bowen was a native of Woodstock and feted his hometown as a countryside retreat from the heat, noise, and smoke of the city.

Bowen hosted four presidents at Roseland Cottage. Its grounds also hold an exquisite parterre garden, an aviary, an icehouse, an impressive carriage house now used for classes and events, and the nation's oldest surviving outdoor bowling alley.

That alone and the story of the presidential visit to that bowling alley are worth the price of a tour. Roseland Cottage is now owned and operated by Historic New England. Tours of the house are available in season, and a number of popular events held through the year give you the opportunity to visit this gem of a dwelling and a glimpse into the unique family who called Roseland Cottage home.

After your visit, continue on and take a well-deserved break at Sweet Evalina's stand, not far from the intersection of Rt. 20. Inside you will learn of the region's effort to revive after World War II by changing the agricultural landscape from cows to potato fields. In those days, each farm would have a fryer at the farm stand and paper bags for the fresh fried chips they offered.

Sweet Evalina's offers ice cream, but also sandwiches and provisions to take on your continuing journey. Their outdoor pavilion offers plenty of seating to sit and eat your ice cream with a picturesque view of a pond and a lone house along the shore.

6

THE POST ROAD:

NORTH KINGSTOWN, RHODE ISLAND,
TO MYSTIC, CONNECTICUT

During an arduous day of travel in early October 1704, Miss Sarah Kemble Knight, alone on horseback but for post riders to guide her, had crossed two rivers, and by nightfall, she had reached a more pleasant stretch of the King's Highway outside of present-day North Kingston:

> … the way being smooth and even, the night warm and serene, and the Tall and thick Trees at a distance, especially when the moon glar'd light through the branches, fill'd my Imagination with the pleasant delusion of a Sumptuous city, fill'd with famous Buildings and churches, with their spiring steeples, Balconies, Galleries, and I know not what…

She was roused from her reverie by the post rider's bugle call ahead, which announce that they had arrived at the mail and stagecoach stop where she was to spend the night.

Far from any place resembling a city, Haven's tavern sat in a remote location in what is now North Kingstown. According to Miss Knight's journal, she was very "civilly received, and courteously entertained, in a clean comfortable house." As she relaxed with a mug of warm chocolate, however, sleep would not come for the noise the gathered men of the town made in the tavern room. As was her wont through her travels, Miss Knight penned her more odious experiences in verse, as the poem that she wrote that evening attests:

> I ask thy Aid, O Potent *Rum!*
> *To Charm these wrangling Topers Dum.*
> *Thou has their Giddy Brains possest-*

The man confounded with the Beast-
And I, poor I, can get no rest.
Intoxicate them with thy fumes:
O still their Tongues till morning comes!

Haven's tavern, as her journal indicates, was a popular place and one of those chosen to act as a "post office" for local residents to pick up or send out mail on the coaches. In later years, guides were written for the traveler, with distances between recommended inns and taverns where accommodations could be found. In Thomas Prince's 1832 almanac, he places Haven's tavern as 16 miles from the Arnold House in Pawtuxet, a good day's travel by stagecoach.

Within the decade after that almanac was published, Haven's tavern was destroyed by fire. Knowing of the site's reputation, the land was purchased by William P. Maxwell, who by 1847 had built and established a public house there that soon grew of equal reputation. He ran the tavern for many years. When Maxwell died, the house and property were deeded to Henry Warde Green of East Greenwich. The property at that time included the house, 128 acres, and a "barn, crib, and other buildings." Eventually, the property was broken up and the house converted to a restaurant called the Boxwood House, operated by Stanley and Eva Ciszek. In the mid-1960s, it was renamed the Pagoda Inn and remains one of the region's enduring restaurants.

The Pagoda Inn, built upon the site of the famous Haven's Tavern. (*Photo by the author*)

A short drive south, you will notice a large development now looming behind a lone nineteenth-century farmhouse. These are the remnants of the Reynolds Farm, once one of the largest in the community. An adjacent eighteenth-century house was torn down; then the pastureland and orchards, which had existed as such for many years, were torn up for residential housing—a sign of the town's growing population, but also of the continued loss of its rural identity.

Despite this development, another farm largely untouched by time can be found nearby. A left on to Richard Smith Drive brings the traveler to Smith's Castle, one of the most historic places in the state of Rhode Island.

Situated on a great lawn above Mill Cove, the large Georgian-style house took its present form after renovations in 1740. Its origins, however, date back to 1678 when Richard Smith, Jr., built a salt box-type house with twin gables and a long, slanted roof in 1678, two years after the Narragansett warriors had burned down his father's blockhouse during King Philip's War.

The history of the site goes back even further, to 1637, when Canonicus, the sachem of the Narragansett, "laid out the boundaries" of the site where Roger Williams established a popular trading post. Those boundaries included a natural spring and an island offshore where William's was asked to keep his goats. These are still part of the property today.

Smith's Castle is the site of the trading post of Roger Williams and the Richard Smith house, situated on a cove outside of Wickford. (*Photo by the author*)

The farm had several transformations over the years, being the northernmost of the Narragansett Plantations when Daniel Updike, a descendant of Smith, inherited the house and remodeled it to serve his large farm. The property at that time encompassed some 3,000 acres over five farms. The "Homestead Farm," as the property was called, held in excess of 500 acres alone.

With a decline in family fortunes, the house was sold and became a humbler, self-sustaining farm through a number of generations. Land was sold off and production from the lands diminished until Alice Babbit Fox inherited the farm. Alice had grown up on the farm, and later married wealthy New Yorker Austin Fox. The couple returned to the homestead and converted the farm into one of the largest dairy concerns in the state. They bred their own brand of cattle, importing Ayrshire cattle from Scotland to breed the Cocumscussoc Ayrshire, whose milk production for a time was the highest in New England. Summer field days were held on the farm each year between 1926 and 1935, a highlight of the Ayrshire Cattle Breeders Association when dairy farmers throughout New England would visit the farm.

Today, the existing house museum offers informative tours of the house, with further information offered on trails that were once farm roads or specific sites of interest, including a path to a natural spring mentioned in the 1651 deed from Roger Williams to Richard Smith. Smith's Castle offers four major events each year, as well as author readings and other adult and family-oriented programs offered throughout the season.

A bronze plaque in stone across Post Road attests to Roger Williams's significance in the area, and a small shaded area owned by the state, which was once a popular rest stop, still bears the designation of Richard Smith's Grove

Just off the Grove is the Palmer Northrup House, which historic architect Norman Isham described as "a veritable stone-end house, it seems of the Providence type." Evidence suggests that the original was a large one-room structure, which was enlarged around 1709. The house features a large fireplace, an ancient summer beam, and at one time the sheathing of some of the earliest homes built in the state.

The Hall family owned the house for many years and a family cemetery lies on the property. Palmer Northrup, for whom the house is named, was a relatively late owner. Local historian Col. Hunter C. White, in his book *North Kingstown and its Old Houses*, believed that the home's proximity to Cocumscussoc Brook was aligned in some way with Smith's Castle and its property. This, along with Isham's description of a Providence-style house, led to speculation that Roger Williams may have built the original structure as his own residence.

Farther along the road, at the intersection of Rt. 1A, the current Wilson Park was once pastureland for the Cocumscussoc Dairy, and it was later used as a ball field in the post-Civil War era when baseball teams began to assemble. Wickford had its own team and played visiting teams at the field. It was so successful that Austin Fox built an ice-cream stand at the site where Wickford Hardware now stands. When the family sold the restaurant in the 1930s, it became one of the first Howard Johnson restaurants in the region.

The Old Post Road, according to North Kingstown Historian Tim Cranston, left the present U.S.1 just after what is now the Shady Lea Historical District at the intersection of Silver Spring Road, and followed Pendar Road to Shermantown Road, leaving the town from there.

Often, the remnants of the old route are posted along U.S.1 as the "Old Post Road", and while in some instances these are simply remaining turnarounds or brief diversions, in other places, they hold small pockets of history preserved in time. In other instances, the route long designated as Scenic Route 1A follows the old route.

Stewart H. Holbrook, when writing his book *The Old Post Road* as part of the McGrath-Hill publishers' *The American Trails* series in 1962, vented his frustration on trying to reconstruct the original route: "… and it was here, either in Wickford, or maybe in North Kingstown, that things, or at least geography, began to go to pieces."

There are long stretches between here and into Connecticut, as Holbroke wrote:

> …it is a matter of on again off again. Much of the way the actual centers of the old towns are not on the turnpike, and can be reached only by leaving it at this or that exit, (called "gates" on the old time pikes) and driving anywhere from a mile or so to 10 miles over highways that may once have been portions of US 1 or even of the Boston Post Road.

Rather than lead the traveler along all these diversions, including sections along U.S.1 that literally demand that you make a U-turn to access Rt. 1A again in the right direction to continue your journey, I will only recommend those diversions off U.S.1 that are worth following the old route and have easy access again to the highway.

With that in mind, we will follow the route parallel to the old off branch, and turn left on to Scenic 1A, which brings us into historic district of Wickford, Rhode Island. Established by Lodowick Updike between 1709 and 1715, the town historically was named "Wickford" in honor of Connecticut Governor John Winthrop's wife who had been a great friend to Richard Smith, Jr., and his wife, Esther. The more popular name "Updike's Newtown" remained its moniker to the end of the eighteenth century. A Revolutionary War diary I recently transcribed refers consistently to the name when describing coming and going from what we now call Wickford Village.

The blocks of historic houses in the town represent a well-preserved colonial and early nineteenth-century community. I recommend travelers who wish to visit the village seek out copies of local historian G. Timothy Cranston's books on walks through Wickford. Cranston has written his column "The View from Swamptown" in the local *Independent* newspaper for the past twenty years. His meticulously detailed histories of the houses in town and the people who lived within them truly bring you back to an earlier time to what was once an industrious and bustling seaside community.

Today, the silent remnants of that time are part of the village's charm. A pair of good restaurants on the water, eclectic shopping, or an opportunity for a kayak excursion are for the offering. A good walking tour is now provided by Histwick, the local historical society, in the way of informative signs that include much of the village's history as well as displaying original work by local artists.

The village is also the site of the Hussey Bridge. The steel double-arched span was recently restored to near pristine condition. It was named for Charles C. Hussey, the first state-appointed bridge engineer, when it was opened in 1925.

Continue across the Hussey Bridge on to Scenic Route 1A. From the original Post Road, an old branch route continued approximately quarter-mile south of the present road through what is Boston Neck, the birthplace of the famed horse, the Narragansett Pacer.

On those pasturelands that grew between Narragansett Bay and the Narrow River, Boston men invested in lands and in breeding a sure-footed, high-stepping riding horse that was tailor-made for the hilly New England country. William Brenton, John Hull, and, later, the Gardiners and Robinsons all held property on the Neck and bred the Pacers, which remained popular in New England until the advent of the stagecoach, when there were fewer individual riders. The Pacer was more profitably exported to the West Indies where it was a favored riding breed of the owners of the large sugar plantations on the islands.

Slaves were also brought to the Caribbean from Rhode Island ports, especially Newport, Bristol, and Warren, though Providence held most of the trade during and after the Revolutionary War. The Pacers bred on Boston Neck and on other farms, and the profits made from their breeding, were ultimately and inextricably tied within the economy of the infamous "triangle trade," of which Rhode Island was a prime provider of rum and horses.

As money from the trade flowed into the state, merchant trading and an increase in the demand for all manner of goods increased the coffers of investors and gave the merchant class increased wealth by the mid-eighteenth century.

During that period, great farms and wealthy estates grew along Boston Neck. One of these was the Rome Farm. A 900-acre estate along Narragansett Bay in North Kingstown, the land was first owned by a British rope manufacturer and privateer speculator named Henry Collins. His loss in privateering ventures led to his selling the land to another British businessman, George Rome.

Rome had ventured in the whaling industry, and by the time that he purchased the estate from Collins in 1760, he was a wealthy man. Once in his ownership, the entrepreneur was determined to build a great estate, complete with formal gardens that he hoped would be among the finest in New England. To that end, he ordered specimens of landscape plantings from England, including some rare varieties, as well as Boxwood Trees.

While the estate acquired the reputation Rome had hoped for, the owner became infamous as a Tory by the outbreak of the American Revolution. Rome was jailed and expelled from the colonies. His estate was seized and was sold at auction to John Carter Brown of Providence, who then resold the estate to Judge Ezekial Gardiner.

Gardiner turned the estate into one of the largest dairy concerns in South County. The family owned the farm through several generations from 1780–1853. Around this time, the farm was purchased from the Gardiners by David Greene and his son, Reynolds Greene. The great manor house that Henry Collins had built and that Rome had expanded burned down during this period. The Greene's built a new house at another location on the property, leaving the foundation, surrounded by box trees, intact.

Today, the estate is the John H. Chafee Nature Preserve along Boston Neck Road. More commonly known as "Rome Point," visitors can walk trails that lead to the shoreline and a fine view of the nearby Jamestown Bridge. It holds an extensive rocky beach with a sheltered inlet called Bissel Cove and a view of Fox Island just offshore.

The preserve is a popular place for dog walkers, so visitors should be prepared to meet many along your way to and from the shore. Most are well behaved and friendly, but not all owners obey leash laws when bringing their dogs to the preserve.

Just across the road from Rome's estate is a far humbler home in the birthplace of famed American portrait artist Gilbert Stuart. The three-story gambrel-roofed house was constructed in 1751 on the bank of the Mattatuxet Brook, which flows into the 57-acre Carr Pond. The mill on the property and its proximity to the ancient Snuff Mill Road are remnants of the period when Stuart's father ran his mill, the first such mill in the country, grinding dried tobacco leaves into the snuff that was popular among the higher social circles.

A gristmill with a fitted water wheel was established nearby as early as 1757. Benjamin Hammond and his family would operate the mill from 1813–1867. The mill today is restored and on the property for visitors to inspect, as

The Gilbert Stuart Museum contains a house museum, the gristmill, and an art gallery. (*Photo by the author*)

is a 1730 English snuff mill, closely resembling the one Stuart's father would have operated.

The young boy who would become an artist was born in the mill house in 1755, and he would leave with his family for Newport six years later.

Today, the house is a fine museum dedicated to the man who would portray Washington and many other colonial luminaries on canvas. A modern, tastefully designed welcome center holds an art gallery and gift shop, as well as hosting special events and lectures through the year. Kayak tours of adjoining Carr Pond are available during the summer and fall seasons.

As we continue along Rt. 1A, existing farms from the colonial era come into view. The first on the right, with its wood-shingled, cupola-topped barn, is a private residence. Another larger estate just down the road is the Casey Farm.

The farmland was purchased in 1702 by Joseph Morey of Jamestown, Rhode Island. He gave the land to his daughter, Mary, after her marriage to Daniel Coggeshall. The Coggeshall family were among the earliest settlers of Newport, though not by design. James Coggeshall had originally immigrated to Boston in 1632 and became an official in the puritan government. His refusal to join in the persecution of Quakers and people of other denominations caused him to lose his position and be banished to Rhode Island, the colony derisively written off as "rogue Island" by Massachusetts officials of the time.

Casey Farm (1750). Built by the Coggeshall family, it came into the Casey family by marriage, and the family continued to own the property into the 1950s. Courtesy of Historic New England. (*Photo by the author*)

Once he entered Rhode Island, James Coggeshall converted to the Quaker theology and raised his family among the Friends in the meetinghouse in Narragansett. On Mary Coggeshall's death in 1724, the lands became the property of Daniel Coggeshall, Jr. He and his wife, Mary Wanton Coggeshall, would build the mansion house that remains on Casey Farm today.

Constructed in 1750, the gambrel-on-hip roof is a design that was seen more often in Newport trader's homes or the master's house on a Caribbean plantation of the same period. The mansion house was at once a prominent landmark on Boston Neck. Rising from the crest of a hill 135 feet above sea level, it is easily noticeable from the West Passage of Narragansett Bay, just beyond Casey Point. The close proximity to Newport gave the farm a ready market for goods to be shipped from the second largest port in the colonies. The Casey Farm, as with the Planters, produced great quantities of Narragansett cheese, as well as staples of corn, wheat, rye, and barley for the West Indian plantations.

Sloops or other cargo-carrying vessels would come up the Narrow River, fill their holds with goods from the farms, and return through Pettasquamscutt Cove and the Narrows to Narragansett Bay.

Daniel Coggeshall, Jr., managed the farm until 1772. Benjamin Gardiner managed the farm from sometime in 1774 until March 1783.

During this period of the Revolutionary War, the Kentish Guard of East Greenwich and other militia were assigned to guard the shoreline along the

West Passage of Narragansett Bay, a task that became increasingly difficult after the British occupation of Newport began in December 1776.

In August 1777, a British ship patrolling the passage caught sight of a group of rebels drilling near the house. They set the ship's guns and fired in their direction and sent a contingent of soldiers ashore. In the ensuing skirmish, one man was killed and a number of militiamen wounded. A bullet hole from a musket ball that passed through a door in the entry hall remains today.

On Daniel Coggeshall Jr.'s death in 1775, his daughter, Abigail, along with her husband, Silas Casey, received a one-eighth share of the property. A successful merchant from East Greenwich, Casey had purchased the remainder of the property by 1781.

Upon Silas Casey's death in 1781, a portion of the farm was deeded to his son, Wanton Casey. The younger Casey was a Revolutionary War veteran, and then had been sent to France by his father to learn French and eventually become a partner in the mercantile business his father had established. He was also one of the founders after the war of the settlement of Marietta on the Ohio River, a town that boasted many veterans from Massachusetts and Rhode Island.

While there, he married Elizabeth Goodale, and in 1793, the couple returned to Rhode Island. The war had so devastated the economy that Casey was forced to find tenants for the farm; he built a house on the prominent corner of Main Street and Division Road (where the post office was latter built), where he and his wife raised ten children.

The large cattle barn and outbuildings presently on the property are dated to the mid-nineteenth century when the farm was managed by Wanton's son, Thomas Goodale Casey. Grandson Thomas Lincoln Casey would oversee the farm during the early twentieth century, though often from afar, as his career in the military would lead him to be Chief of Engineers for the United States Army Corp of Engineers, and the oversight of the completion of the Washington Monument. On the farm, he would hire the stoneworkers who built the massive stone walls along the property after the rerouting of Boston Neck Road in the 1930's. The old Boston Neck Road is still walkable as trail maintained by the farm for their summer camp programs. The farm today remains a working farm under management of Historic New England. A popular outreach program allows classrooms throughout Rhode Island to incubate eggs and hatch chicks that will be returned to the farm and raised among the heritage breeds of Rhode Island Reds and Dominique chickens.

Casey Farm also hosts a children's summer camp and a farmer's market each Saturday as part of the Coastal Growers Association. Tours of a portion of the mansion house, the adjacent barns and outbuildings, and the farm itself are available during the season.

Continue along Boston Neck Road to South Ferry Road. A quick detour to the historic South Ferry Church is worth a visit. The docks at South Ferry were used by a number of the Narragansett Planters, whose farms resided on the Neck, including the Hazard and Robinson families. A large mural, originally painted for the Saunderstown Post Office during the W.P.A., depicts the loading of goods on to ships at the dock, including cattle and Narragansett Pacers, as well as grains and barrels of mutton being loaded by black and indigenous slaves. The mural is now in the collection of the South County History Center in Kingston, Rhode Island.

The next stretch of road contains a congested area as we approach Bonnet Shores, the lengthy stretch of calm beach that lies inland and west of Bonnet Point. It is a favorite for families with young children, a place we visited each summer when I was a child and explored the seemingly endless shoreline. If you would like to visit the beach, take a left on Bonnet Shores Road and then a right on to Bonnet Point Road and follow it down to Bonnet Shores Beach and Kelley Beach.

Continue on Rt. 1A as the road curves right past Annawan Drive. You will notice a turn off on the right for Old Boston Neck Road, a leftover byway from the days that the route was diverted for taverns and entertainment. It rejoins and crosses the present route less than a quarter-mile down the road.

A concrete and stone bridge crosses the Pettasquamscutt River just before it reaches the cove on your right. Continue on Boston Neck Road and you will shortly see the waters of Little Neck Pond on the right, and just ahead, the towers from the casino that once stood adjacent to the seawall of the Narragansett town beach.

Constructed between 1883 and 1886, the unique design of the stone twin towers and porte-cochere archway leading to the casino built in Victorian shingle-style architecture, the resort was an immediate destination. It offered gilded age visitors a variety of restaurants, and besides the casino, it held a theater, a ballroom, a bandstand, and recreation in the form of boating, tennis, shooting, and bowling. A large beach pavilion that mimicked the style of the casino was also erected.

The Narragansett Pier Casino rivaled those at Newport, and it was often the preferred destination for those who arrived on their own yachts and sought to avoid crowded Newport Harbor. By the 1890s, the casino, adjacent hotels, and the shoreline led *Harper's Weekly* to exclaim "the beach … is the center of life in Narragansett."

On September 12, 1900 disaster struck the pier and neighboring buildings when the "Great Fire" erupted in the nearby Rockingham Hotel and quickly consumed most of the village's center. All that remained of the casino was its granite foundation and the stone towers we still see today. The towers were first restored in 1910, with a new roof and replacement of the wooden interior as well.

A second casino was built on the site of the old Rockingham Hotel in 1905. This lasted as a public casino through the years, and it became immensely popular during the Depression era and into the 1940s when dance bands and swing music was the frequent entertainment. This structure, too, fell victim to fire, burning to the ground on May 29, 1956. The Towers, as they are called today, are still the gateway to Narragansett pier and are used for events and weddings throughout the year.

The popular seawall that lines the rocky shoreline of the Narragansett Town Beach was constructed after the 1938 hurricane devastated the privately-owned shoreline. The town purchased the beachfront and constructed the seawall and two town-operated bathing pavilions on the beach. The State of Rhode Island would likewise claim parts of the shoreline in the storm's aftermath and turn beachfronts at Galilee and Scarborough into popular public beaches.

You may continue on Ocean Road from here to visit the state beaches along the shoreline to Point Judith, or to continue on our journey into Connecticut, take a right onto South Pier Road to travel back to U.S. Rt. 1.

Follow South Pier Road beyond the overpass of R. 1, where it becomes Woodruff Road. Look for the sign directing you to Rt. 1 and take a left on Salt Pond Road, which will lead to the ramp of Rt. 1 South, toward Westerly. From here, the four-lane highway leads for several miles down to Matunuck, past Perryville, and into Charlestown.

Along this stretch of the old highway during stagecoach days were wide expanses of farmlands as the carriages rambled past great plantations and farms containing thousands of acres right down to the shore.

One such large estate was the farm of General Joseph Stanton, which lies on the Old Post Road adjacent to Rt. 1.

Here in Charlestown, the Stanton family built its own small empire between bordering colonies beginning with land given to Thomas Stanton in 1655 where he built the beginnings of the great house, which is the third oldest

The General Joseph Stanton House (1655, 1740), now the Stanton Inn on Old Post Road in Charlestown, Rhode Island. (*Photo by the author*)

structure in Rhode Island. Stanton had originally founded a trading business with William Whiting at Hartford, Connecticut, where the pair created a monopoly on the fur trade. After Whiting's death in 1647, "Stanton moved to the border region between Rhode Island and Connecticut where, in 1650, he was granted control of the fur trade along the Pawcatuck River," as written in Bernard Bailyn's *The New England Merchants in the Seventeenth Century.*

His son, Daniel, would move to Barbados to act as the "overseas partner" with the family firm. Thomas Stanton & Sons shipped corn, beans, dried fish, jerked venison, salt, and flour to Barbados aboard two vessels, the *Alexander and Martha*, built by Daniel in 1681, and an older vessel built by his brother, Thomas Stanton, Jr. The sloops returned to Pawcatuck laden with sugar, molasses, and rum, as well as the occasional slave, according to one Connecticut historian, "only 3–4 each year." As with other New England colonies, these West Indian slaves would have been integrated among the indigenous and African slaves already bound on southern New England plantations.

Thomas Stanton died in 1677. His son, Daniel, would die sometime before 1688 in Barbados, leaving a wife and child. Thomas Stanton's nephew, Joseph Stanton, would inherit the Rhode Island farm and expand the house, adding the last addition around 1740, by which time the farm had become a large dairy concern. Stanton also built a house of his own in 1739 on a low bluff overlooking the family's horse breeding grounds that stretched beyond to Quonochontaug pond and to the shoreline of Block Island Sound. His son, Joseph Stanton, Jr., would be born in the family home on July 19, 1739. He continued the family tradition of entering the military, being commissioned as a second lieutenant in the Rhode Island regiment raised for the expedition against Canada during the French and Indian war in 1759.

Stanton went on to a political career and served in the General Assembly from 1768–1755. His estate and wealth grew considerably, so that an old account attests that "He owned a lordship in Charlestown, a tract of four miles long and two miles wide, kept 40 horses, as many slaves, and made a great dairy."

In modern times, the sprawling colonial was transformed into an inn, opening the house to the public for the first time, and a spate of ghostly encounters in its rooms and corridors. As such incidents accumulated over the years, the house has drawn paranormal investigators and psychics to its doors. I have not seen much evidence found by these investigations, but I have seen, while interviewing the owner some years back, a photograph taken by a guest in which, through a doorway, can be seen an epaulette on the shoulder of a military uniform as though an officer is strolling past.

Continue on Rt. 1 South, past Ninigret Park, and bear right at the intersection with Rt. 1A. As you cross Airport Road, Rt. 1 becomes Franklin

Street in Westerly. On the right, as you approach School Street, is the Babcock-Smith house museum, an elegant Georgian manor house built around 1734.

As you reach Granite Street, a few older houses and then grander homes appear on the left, and on the right, just past the intersection of Grove Avenue, is the expanse of beautiful Wilcox Park.

Continue to follow Rt. 1, now Broad Street as it passes the public library, one of a number of notable historic buildings in town. Cross the bridge at the Pawcatuck River, visible on the left, and follow Broad Street to West Broad Street and under an overpass and past the junction of Rt. 2 on the right, to continue straight toward the village of Stonington.

Bear left to stay on Rt. 1 as you approach the old village common with its war monuments on the right. You will drive past a mix of old and modern housing, then through a slightly congested business district, the Post Office, modern condominiums, and non-descript business parks and offices. Continue past the large V.F.W. hall and the intersection of Spellman Drive.

Continue on Rt. 1 until the intersection of Rt. 1A and a pleasant diversion. Bear left on to Rt. 1A and continue on this road until it bears right. At this junction, continue straight toward the center of the village. Cross an extended, above-ground bridge past an old mill repurposed as a brewery, and then bear left onto Water Street.

Park on this upper end of the street before the road narrows as it enters the historic district with its attractive clutter of shops and restaurants. Grand houses also line the street, especially as you near Stonington Point and the old lighthouse.

This stone citadel and attached lighthouse was constructed in 1840 when it replaced an earlier wooden structure at a site that had great importance in the eighteenth and nineteenth century in guiding ships across the treacherous waters of Fisher Island Sound. It was originally built with a flat roof and simulated battlements, but a gable roof was added just two years later and the structure became what we still see today.

The lighthouse was home to seven keepers and their families until 1889 when the beacon was supplanted by beacons installed on the harbor breakwaters. The keeper for those lights lived in the house until 1909.

The lighthouse was abandoned after a new keeper's house was built adjacent to the old one, and in 1925, the Stonington Historical Society purchased the property from the United States government. Two years later, it was opened as the nation's first lighthouse museum.

Today, the lighthouse remains a fascinating repository of memorabilia of Stonington's maritime history, the journeys of her sea captains, and as well as artifacts from the British attack of the town in 1814.

I visited the museum and Stonington Point on a pleasant afternoon in late summer. I especially enjoyed lounging on the grounds after taking in the

Stonington Lighthouse (1840) protected the ships traveling through Fisher Island Sound until 1889. (*Photo by the author*)

museum exhibits, and the view across Little Narragansett Bay to Watch Hill and Napatree Point on the Rhode Island shore. The museum had a model of the steamship *Rhode Island* among its collection, and items from the days when it plied the waters from Watch Hill to Stonington harbor. One of Stonington's sea captains highlighted in the museum is Capt. Nathaniel Brown Palmer, whose house is nearby and worth a visit.

Born into a seafaring family, Palmer took his first voyage at fourteen with a seal-hunting crew, as did many other young men from Stonington in that era. He was soon captain of a small sloop that served as the exploratory vessel for a fleet of sealers. During a voyage in 1820 in which his sloop covered some 100,000 miles, he sighted the Antarctic Peninsula in mid-November, an area that would be calmed Palmer Land thereafter.

Palmer later designed the prototype of the clipper ship while on a trade visit to China. When he returned to Stonington, Palmer had the vessel built to his design, and the following year, the *Houqua* sailed from New York City to Canton, China, in just ninety-five days.

The Nathaniel B. Palmer house (1852–54) is an elegant hip-roofed dwelling with a gable in the center of each façade and an octagonal cupola that provides

The Nathaniel B. Palmer House, Stonington. Palmer began his life at sea as a seal hunter and navigator in the Antarctic. (*Photo by the author*)

a 360-degree view. The main entrance is framed by four Corinthian columns supporting the flat portico roof above the doorway, which is flanked by a pair of paneled pilasters.

The interior holds exquisite wood and marble work throughout. I was especially envious of the captain's den, with built-in bookshelves and cabinets and mahogany-veneered paneled doors.

Docents from the Stonington Historical Society conduct tours of the house on Friday–Monday afternoons during the summer season into fall.

Continue on Rt. 1A until you reach the intersection of Stonington Road, and take a left to rejoin Rt. 1 South. You quickly pass the edge of Lambert's Cove, a protected inlet above Stonington harbor. Up ahead, you will cross a small concrete bridge over the end of Collins Cove, and then the longer bridge over the Pawcatuck River.

As you cross the bridge and head the rough the intersection of Cove Road, look for the grand old colonial farm on the right. The road continues as a pleasant country two-lane drive. Drive past the intersection of Old Stonington Road on the right and continue through a congested section of retail plazas and businesses. As you approach the Town of Mystic, you will cross another bridge a pleasant stretch of the Pequotsepos River, and on the left an ancient burial ground lain on its southern bank.

Continue straight past the intersection with Denison Avenue, bear right at the next intersection, and then left as you reach the Civil War monument, encircled within an oval by a small iron fence to form a rotary. Drive past the large white Congregational Church and parsonage, through the intersection of Willow Street, and on into the heart of Mystic.

If you find yourself in a line of cars, you are headed for the Mystic drawbridge. The formal name of the structure is the Mystic River Bascule Bridge, and it was constructed by the J. L. Fitzgerald Construction Company in 1820 after a design by Thomas Ellis Brown. The bridge has a length of 218 feet and is 85 feet wide. It has an 85-foot moveable span, and it employs two 250-short-ton concrete-filled counterweights to lift the span and allow ships to pass. Few, as one might imagine, pass the bridge these days. More commonly seen are the kayakers out for a river paddle or the slow-boat cruises that leave the dock by the riverside restaurants.

Cross the bridge and prepare to spend some time in downtown Mystic. My tip is to continue straight through town, then bear left at Bank Square, just past the modern brick building that holds the bookshop, and park in one of the public lots at the top of the hill to the left, across from the large brick mill building with the sign Factory Square.

The village grew into a major shipbuilding seaport in the nineteenth century and is home to the largest maritime museum in Old Mystic Village and Mystic Seaport. The boatyard at Mystic Seaport remains the premiere shop for museums and private owners to send their historic vessels for restoration. Most recently, the seaport celebrated the completed restoration of the *Charles W. Morgan*, the last wooden whaling vessel in the United States.

Mystic remains one of my favorite coastal villages, with access to kayaks, boat cruises along the river, shops and restaurants enough to fill more than a day of browsing and eating, and historic houses and the seaport that remain attractions for visitors throughout the summer into fall.

I have never felt crowded in the village. A walk away from the shops to view the elegant sea captains' homes that face the Mystic River along Gravel street, or crossing the bridge to find the small park on the other bank (off Cottrell Street), can take one to places that are far removed from the retail shops and restaurants, the clatter of restaurant wares, and loud conversation.

Bank Square Books has hosted me several times as histories that I have written have been published. It became my habit to spend the weekend in town, and I encourage the reader to do the same.

7

THE DURHAM ROAD:

GUILFORD TO DURHAM, CONNECTICUT

Guilford is one of Connecticut's earliest coastal settlements, having been established on land purchased in 1639 from Wequash Cooke, a native sachem who allied himself with Uncas and the English during the Pequot War; he was one of the few Native American leaders to convert to Christianity and adapt an English surname.

Being such an early settlement, Guilford is considered to have the third largest collection of historic houses of any community in New England. Five are historic house museums, all within a short walk or drive from one another, and definitely worth taking the time to visit.

The Henry Whitfield House (1640) was built as a stone garrison, one of five other stone houses built in the region as protective "forts" for residents in the event of an attack from Native Americans, and as shelter for travelers as well. Built from local granite, the house reminded me at once of the stone garrisons I had seen built along the Mohawk Valley during those years of the Indian Wars.

The walls of the house are nearly 2 feet thick, the mortar that binds them together made of yellow clay and crushed oyster shells, an early method of mortaring that was similar to the mix used for the stone-enders in Providence. The frame was hewn of solid oak timbers and white pine used for partitions inside the house.

Settlers built the house as a home for Minister Henry Whitfield, his wife, Dorothy, and their nine children. Having begun construction late in 1639, only part of the "great hall" and a fireplace on the north side of the house were barely finished before winter set in. By the summer of 1640, the hall, a second floor, and attic were completed, and the family was able to take up residence.

The Henry Whitfield House (1639), the oldest house in Guilford, was built as a home for the town minister, a meetinghouse, and a stone fort for early citizens. (*Photo by the author*)

The house served as the first meetinghouse and church in the community. In 1860, a Roman Catholic parish met in the house before St. George's church was built along the town green.

The Whitfield House would house a succession of owners after 1659. After Whitfield's death, the town desired to purchase the house from his widow to be used as a grammar school but failed to come up with sufficient funds. The house was then sold to a London merchant, and thereafter housed a succession of owners until 1900, when it was officially sold to the town for $8,500.

It became the state of Connecticut's first museum in 1899, and three years later underwent another remodeling under the guidance of Norman Isham, the noted Rhode Island historical architect who would work on numerous historical houses that still bear his imprint today. The house remains a fascinating museum, both for its varied collection and as an early example of a house museum in New England.

Two other historic houses are within walking distance on Boston Road: the Hyland-Wildman house (1713), an early salt box house with a framed overhang, and the Thomas Burgis II house (1735), a two and a half-story, five-over four-bay windowed clapboarded house with a central chimney. Burgis was a successful shoemaker in town and operated a tannery as well. His house was extended to a salt box configuration in 1800 and remains a fine example of the style. The house was remodeled in 1990 after some years of neglect, and it was listed on the National Registry of Historic Places in 2000.

Leaving the center of Guilford via Church Street, just opposite the north end of the town green, cross Rt. 1, the Old Boston Post Road, and continue north past a Middle School and underneath a bridge for the Connecticut Turnpike on to Rt. 77, the stretch of road that was long known as the Guilford and Durham Turnpike. Constructed under charter in 1824, the road was improved and often called the "Stagecoach Road" by locals, though its origins date back to the early 1700s.

The ride ahead offers long stretches of farmland and rural countryside. The road runs parallel to a short stretch of the West River just past Prospect Hill Road and disappears and reappears intermittently for the next 13 miles. Along the sections where the river runs close to the road are patchwork parking spaces for fisherman.

At about the 5.5-mile mark, you will reach the intersection of Rt. 80, or "The Old Toll Road," which had its origins in 1818 as the Pettipauge and Guilford Turnpike, running from the Madison and Guilford line northeast to Killington, then to Deep River, at the edge of New London county. Another turnpike was constructed in 1824, running from Fairhaven and intersecting with the toll road to Killingworth Center. The present Rt. 80 was established in 1932 when the state renumbered the highways.

Cross the intersection and continue on Rt. 77. You will soon come to the Dudley Farm Museum. The attractive house was built in 1845 by Erastus Dudley on land his family had owned for a least a generation before his obtaining the farm. Dudley prospered as a farmer in what was then North Guilford and established a tannery and gristmill along the West River where it ran through his property.

The Federal Revival house, with a large ell, hosts a tasteful reproduction of a 1900 farmhouse, whose furnishings and collected artifacts give the history of the home's inhabitants.

A large barn, which evolved during three separate stages of the farm's life, now holds a large collection of tools and farm equipment from the era. The adjacent outbuildings and gardens are a pleasant walk through the early twentieth-century landscape of a New England farm. Beyond, you will find heritage breed cattle grazing in pastures and an abundance of sheep. The Dudley Farm Museum gives tours through the summer, as well as offering special programs through the season.

The farm also serves as part of Dudley Barrows Woods, a 95-acre section of woodlands that connect with lands of the historic Barrow Farm as part of the Guilford Land Trust. Trails through the main section of the woods lead to three granite knobs known as "The Three Monks."

Continue north on the Durham Road. Be mindful of traffic intersecting from roads east and west, especially Skylark Drive from the southeast and the more open intersection of County Road from the west. A popular country store and deli lie ahead on the left-hand side of the road. This would be your last opportunity to get a meal to go for some distance.

The Durham Road continues to snake through some of the best well-preserved farm and woodlands in the state of Connecticut. Eventually, you will reach a more built-up area as you reach the southern tip of the mile-long Lake Quonnipaug, the literal Qunnipiac word for "long pond." The vast, 98.7-acre body of water is in an area originally known as Cohabit, and the first purchase of the area from the indigenous people occurred around 1686.

Within a decade, plots were divided and land was parceled out to investors from Guilford. Mostly farmers, the men were known to spend the week clearing their parcel, living together in crudely made cabins, and then returning home before the Sabbath; thus the name first given to the site.

The area would become North Guilford and remain sparsely inhabited and an agricultural community until the early twentieth century, when vacation homes began to be built away from Guilford's shoreline. In 1929, the Land and Lake Development Company built the Guilford Lake Estates, creating a chain of three artificial lakes with vacation homes around them.

Today, the largest natural lake in the region is still a popular boating destination. In recent years, residents and the state have had to battle the growth of invasive plants as with many other waterways in New England. Unfortunately, this often involves chemicals that could harm the ecosystem of the pond itself, namely fish and turtles that live among its quiet eddies and coves. A beach can be found just off Rt. 77, and at the northern tip of Lake Quonnipaug is a boat launch for small craft, including kayak and canoe.

Continue north along Durham Road (Rt. 77) and in several miles you will reach the intersection of Rt. 17, another old road that is still known as the New Haven Road. Rt. 77 now becomes Rt. 17, and just above this intersection, the road is intersected again from the southeast by Rt. 79. These all join Rt. 17 North and your arrival in the Durham Historic District is just up the road.

The Durham Historic District is a rare gem of authentic colonial structures preserved in a rural New England setting. The houses, barns, and schools stretch along a good portion of Main Street. I would suggest the visitor find a parking space on Town House Road, in the loop that forms around the common, and walk as much as you can from there.

The public library is located just off this parking area, across Maple Avenue. The staff can provide you with a well written and produced walking guide of the historic district, which I found extremely helpful as a starting point to researching the houses ad their inhabitants. On the Townhouse Road itself are several structures moved to the area from other parts of town to enhance the walking tour.

The town green was established in 1707, but as the pamphlet points out, it was a very different site from the clover-filled swath of lawn. Cattle were initially grazed on the green, and as early as 1730, five "haywards" were assigned to keep the fences in good repair to keep the cows from wandering. The Congregational Meeting house was constructed in 1737 and remained on the northeast corner until 1835. Public notices were nailed on a board outside the front door, and "There was probably more dirt than grass, due to the constant traffic humans, horses, and the hogs and geese the town allowed to run free." That same year, two schools were established in the village: the Union School, built across the intersection from the New Haven Road, and the North School, built at the upper end of Main Street.

When the Sabbath house and stables nearby were torn down in 1835, however, the town green became similar to what we see today. It was considered the "gem" of the town in a Victorian travel guide, and as in most New England towns, it became the focus of holiday ceremonies and celebrations for the community. It remains that way today with a Veteran's Memorial at the south end, and it is large enough to host the Durham Agricultural Fair each year.

Adjacent to the present town hall, which was originally the South Congregational Church, are two small buildings that are relics of the town's early history.

The small clapboard "Sabbath day" house comes from those early years of the town's history when all residents per the law in the colony were required to attend Sunday worship services. These services were held each Sunday morning in the village meetinghouse. Worship on Sunday was an all-day affair, with a break at midday for people to return home and eat a hearty meal before returning for afternoon services.

While this routine proved passable in spring and summer, the fall and winter months brought their own challenges to parishioners, with gales and then heavy snow often making traveling cumbersome, especially for those on foot. In addition, early meetinghouses were unheated, and many lived too far from the meetinghouse to return home and warm themselves sufficiently before heading back to worship.

The solution came with these small houses built nearby the meetinghouse. The town meeting authorized the building of Sabbath day houses such as this one in December 1721. Once built, families would send a servant or one of their children ahead of Sunday worship to stoke the stove in the Sabbath day house and prepare the midday meal, so that by the time morning services had ended, a warm house and a hot meal were ready for those congregants who lived far from the meetinghouse.

In the early 1800s, Connecticut law did away with the requirement to attend Sunday services, and wood stoves were installed in most meetinghouses. Sabbath day house became unused and became rundown. Some, like the one on the town green, were removed to other locations and used as housing. The Sabbath day house that sits on the green today was one originally built for worshipers there. It was returned to the green and restored in 1967.

The Center Schoolhouse was originally built just north of the town hall in 1775. An earlier schoolhouse, the first in town, was built around the same location in 1722. While the later structure may seem small, the original schoolhouse measured only 26 feet by 18 feet. The two-story whitewashed clapboard building with ample windows and separate doors for girls and boys was a great improvement over the dark and drab structures built as schoolhouses in previous years.

Despite these poor conditions for learning early on, the town became a center for learning, these efforts led by early Yale-educated minister Nathanial Chauncey. As the town's first minister, he helped to establish the Book Company of Durham, only the second private subscription library in the country. With twenty-five original members, the book collection was housed in a member's home and held volumes on such subjects as history, theology, and philosophy. The subscription library was disbanded in 1865 as the high production of printing made many books more affordable, and a public library to be constructed for the town was approved by voters in 1894. The original library was constructed in 1901 and remains as part of the modern library today.

As you set out for your walk, be mindful that there is limited walking space on the left side of the road heading north. Cross at Maple Street and use the sidewalk on the opposite side of the road. You may want to cross to view some of the historic houses close up, but use caution and, if possible, a zoom lens to take pictures.

One of the first historic houses you will encounter beyond the green is the handsome Federal-style house known as the General James Wadsworth house. The original structure of the house was built in 1755 by Boston native Gilbert Deblois, a merchant who had been banished from Massachusetts; by the time of the American Revolution, he was routed from Durham for his Tory leanings and the house was confiscated by the town.

In 1782, the state of Connecticut granted the house to General Wadsworth *in lieu* of his "civil and military service." Wadsworth added the second story and an ell to create the house that still stands today. Wadsworth was involved in the town's civic affairs for many years, serving as a representative on the Governor's council (an early version of the state legislature), and he served as town clerk and a county judge as well as a major-general in the local militia before the Revolutionary War. After the war, he continued his political

Center Schoolhouse (1775) near town green on Durham Road. (*Photo by the author*)

The house of General James Wadsworth (1755). The house was confiscated from a Tory supporter and given to Wadsworth at the close of the war for his "civic and military service." (*Photo by the author*)

ambitions, and fearful like many at the time of a strong federal government, he was among the majority of Durhamites to oppose the ratification of the United States constitution.

Shortly after, you will cross a traffic bridge above the Allyn Brook before you reach Mill Pond Lane. Although it may seem insignificant, the site was the scene of a great tragedy.

In the winter of 1822, when the Durham Road was a heavily traveled stagecoach route, a 94-foot-long, 21-foot-high wooden span crossed the brook. On the morning of February 21, after a deep freeze had thickened the ice around the brook, a southern storm brought torrential rain and 10 a.m., a flash flood that broke up chunks of ice and sent them careening into the bridges wooden bridge supports, damaging at least one of the span's central beams.

Within the space of an hour, a stagecoach from Middletown arrived in Durham, and despite warnings from a neighbor who had witnessed the flood, the driver drove the stagecoach on to the damaged span. As the horses reached the southern end of the bridge, the structure collapsed, sending the coach, horses, driver, and three passengers into the icy brook below. Two of the passengers were killed, while the stagecoach driver and one passenger survived.

After this incident, the town replaced the wooden span with a graceful stone bridge that served the route for the next century. The modern bridge that crosses the brook today was actually constructed above the old bridge. In 1994, when improvements were made to the highway, it was decided to expose the west side of the old stone bridge and build a catwalk where pedestrians may view the structure up close and admire its craftsmanship. The catwalk may be accessed by crossing Rt. 77 at the crosswalk at the end of the modern bridge.

Before you cross the road, however, take a look at the small house recessed from the road down a long drive just before Mill Pond Lane. This is the Timothy Hall house (*c.* 1750) whose inhabitant had the misfortune of contracting smallpox in 1771. The disease was the scourge of colonial times, ravishing families and diminishing whole communities from outbreaks throughout the eighteenth century. Town officials had approved the building of a "pest house" or hospital in a remote area of town to prevent such devastation from occurring in Durham. Accordingly, the forty-nine-year-old Hall was removed from the house where his six children, ranging in age from six to twenty-two, resided. He died in the pest house on July 29, 1771 and was buried on the grounds, for fear of his body infecting those who would normally have transferred it to the old cemetery across from the house.

The Old Durham cemetery lies on the hillside across the road. After viewing the stone bridge across Allyn Brook, take some time to view the old

The old Durham cemetery lies on the hillside beyond the bridge crossing. (*Photo by the author*)

gravestones on the tree-shaded hill above Durham Road. Dating from 1700, it is the final resting place of many of the town's early inhabitants, both rich and poor. You may find the elaborately carved tombstone of Timothy Hall there. It was placed there by the family after his death, but his remains are still at the site of the old pest house in the shadow of nearby Mount Pisgah.

Cross back at the intersection and continue walking north along Rt. 77. You will pass a few more modern houses, and crossing Pickett Lane, the modern Cognachaug High School. Across the road is a handsome white clapboard church, and on your right, the large eighteenth-century structure is the Lemuel Camp Tavern (*c*. 1795).

Camp built the main part of the house and opened it as a tavern by 1806. The town was growing in industry by this time and several general stores and other shops were constructed nearby around this time.

After his death in 1843, the house was divided among his widow, Martha Pickett Camp, and their two children. His wife, Martha Pickett Camp (of the family Pickett Lane was named for), died in 1860. By the turn of the century, the house had been sold to Sallie B. Strong who it is presumed, added the addition to the house and rented rooms to tenants. The house was restored to its present condition in 1978.

Across the road you will notice a fine example of a Greek Revival house, one of several interspersed between the earlier houses built along Main Street. Continuing on, you will walk past the Durham Volunteer Ambulance Corp garage, built in front of the old Durham Manufacturing Plant, whose founder's handsome Victorian home rests at the top of the drive onto the factory grounds.

Continuing north, you will soon come to the intersection of Wallingford Road (Rt. 68), which has handsome houses on either side.

The handsome gambrel-roofed, double-chimney house facing Wallingford Road is the Spelman Tavern (*c.* 1740). During the Revolutionary War, town officials approached Phineas Spelman about operating a tavern in his large house. He agreed to do so in 1779, appropriating the necessary furnishings for operating an inn, which included nine beds and thirty-eight chairs.

Spelman operated the tavern until he contracted smallpox and the debilitating illness brought about his death in 1783. His widow, Elizabeth, took over the operations of the tavern to support the seven children living in the household. She successfully ran the tavern until 1790, when, with other taverns operating in town, officials declined to renew her operating license.

Elizabeth Spelman appealed to the Connecticut General Assembly, backed by a petition signed by some sixty-five residents of the town testifying that "by industry, prudence & economy she has kept a reputable House." The assembly denied her appeal, and in 1793, she again applied to town officials for a tavern license. By then, there were three other taverns operating in town, and officials worried that "the unnecessary increase of taverns have a Tendency to promote Tavern haunting, occasion mispence of Time and Corrupt the Morals of People." The town then deemed that to grant license for another tavern would be "detrimental to the good order and Morals of inhabitants". The widow Spelman died in 1801, having failed to procure a license for her one-time livelihood.

The Spelman Tavern (1740). Phineas Spelman's house was opened as a tavern and inn at the start of the Revolutionary War. Following his death in 1783, his widow continued to operate the tavern until 1790. (*Photo by the author*)

Just beyond the intersection of Wallingford Road lies the Congregational Church constructed in 1847. The Greek Revival-style church was built after a dispute among the congregants, who built their own church on the north side of Allyn Brook about a half-mile down the road. The remainder of the congregation constructed a new South Congregational Church, which they dedicated in 1849 and which now serves as the town hall. Such feuds among congregants in New England churches were not uncommon. This one was mended by 1886, when the church gathered under one roof again at this location.

At this point in your walking tour of the town, I suggest you head south back to the town green. The surrounding houses around the green and across Durham Road will provide more historical sites to visit, including the large Durham Academy, a private school erected in 1844, and the Moses Austin House (*c.* 1745). A visit to the cemetery accessible by a entry beside the town hall is also worth a visit, with fine Victorian tombstones, obelisks, and mausoleums throughout, and a fine view of the valley lying to the west of town.

The Old Durham Road is also the historic route taken by General George Washington with troops on their way to Cambridge, Massachusetts. On June 29, 1775, Washington and his entourage arrived in Durham after marching from Wallington where he purchased gunpowder. In town, Washington stopped at Mill Hill, located on the east side of Main Street, to meet with General James Wadsworth. He then proceeded to the northern end of town where he spent time at John Swathal's tavern and procured fresh horses.

The Town of Durham contributed 103 men to the American Revolution. In 1777, the town assembled a rationing board. Among the restricted items was salt, then a key component in making gunpowder. That winter, two men from Durham drove a pair of oxen 500 miles to Valley Forge to feed the officers of the general's army.

Washington's next visit came after his inauguration in 1789 when he revisited the town during part of his tour of the states. Nearly two years before, the town had voted by a wide margin to reject the proposed constitution of the United States. As he did in other towns, he likely lobbied the local lawmakers to ratify the document.

Durham's historical district remains a treasure to be leisurely explored. When you are ready to move on, return to your car and continue on Rt. 17 north until just before Middletown and the intersection of Rt. 9. Take a right and head south on 9 until you reach the intersection of Connecticut Rt. 154.

Take the entrance and continue along the route as it follows the Connecticut River.

8

THE GOSHEN—SHARON TURNPIKE:

GOSHEN TO SHARON, CONNECTICUT

Start your drive from Goshen, Connecticut, at the old rotary intersection of Rt. 4 and Old Middle Road, marked as State Highway 63. Take time to explore a bit of the town before you take the turnpike. I parked in the lot of the resplendent white church at the intersection. It is something I have become accustomed to finding in my travels. Very often on these old routes, where there is barely a shoulder to pull off the road, the village church lot provides a place to park. No one has ever complained to me about parking in a church lot, and usually, they are within walking distance of a cluster of historic buildings, just as the church would have been for the villagers that walked or rode horseback to Sunday service.

Just 150 yards from the rotary, the road becomes a quiet country lane. One either side of the road are fine examples of nineteenth-century houses, including the Goshen Historical Society (1842), which was in the process of getting repainted when I stopped by. A large gold painted eagle with outspread wings adorns the front entrance.

Across the road, a large, gold clapboard farmhouse stands, as well as a relic of New England: a genuine general store. The structure looks to be very old; I would date it from the 1820s, and it looks to be nearly sagging from the weight of the variety of goods crammed into its shelves and every nook and cranny.

As you set out on the turnpike, within a short distance you will notice wetlands on either side that are now protected by the Goshen Land Trust. Within a short drive on the right, a handsome white-clapboarded colonial home comes into view. The Mary Stuart House (1798) is a four-bay, central chimney colonial, with an added Victorian porch. The house is now a bed and

Goshen general store, Goshen, Connecticut. (*Photo by the author*)

breakfast, open year-round and with only five guestrooms available, it offers a quiet weekend away.

Further along, we find what I consider a real historical treasure: an old wooden mill set beside the Marshepaug River. The mill was built in the late eighteenth century as manufacturing began to take hold in rural areas. The simple, white duplex across the street may have served as mill housing by the mid-1800s. Bear right to continue on Rt. 4.

This section of the old turnpike has recently been repaved, so the drive was a pleasure compared with so many of the old pikes that are in such disrepair, something Rhode Islanders like myself have sadly accepted for a lifetime, as I reminded myself while rattling along the old Putnam Pike as I started my drive to western Connecticut.

Continue for some distance on Rt. 4, and just past Bartholomew Hill Road. The Sharon Turnpike becomes Bunker Hill Road. As you follow the curve of the road, just around the bend is the entrance to the Mohawk State Forest, which has a beautiful overlook of the distant Berkshire Mountains. It is certainly worth the brief detour just down Toomey Road, straight from the park entrance. There is a quiet picnic area just across the road from the overlook.

At the intersection of Cornwall Hollow Road (Rt. 43), Rt. 4 and Rt. 128, continue straight through the intersection on to Rt. 128 and continue on the route of the old turnpike. This road remains a gem of rural landscapes as

Scenic overlook from Mohawk State Forest. (*Photo by the author*)

fine nineteenth-century homes remain widely separated, and existing farms as well, one with a fine "bank-barn" constructed with a stone foundation built into the slope of the hill below the farmhouse.

Continue on through a heavily wooded area, and just past the intersection on the left with Rt. 129 is a finely crafted stonewall, fronting an early center chimney colonial house. Bearing only three-bay windows in front and three smaller six-paned windows above, vertical four-paned highlights were created within the classic square portal that frames the door.

Another heavily wooded section of roadway follows. Bear left at the intersection as Wright Hill Road enters from the right. Another wooded section of roadway continues. I have always been both amazed and gratified that such stretches of roadway still exist on the east coast. No matter how populated or congested your own location might have become over the years, there are still green roadways, forests, and protected areas within a day's drive to leave those stresses behind.

As you approach Cornwall, a few modern homes and the Cornwall Fire Station come to view. Within a short distance, a long, white-picket fence runs parallel to the roadway, the nineteenth-century house on the old estate nearly hidden from view by the boughs of the tall pines overhanging the fence. As you continue, you will notice on the right, a long stonewall of another estate, whose mansion house rests on a hill above the road, just barely visible, with its tall white center chimney. A newer house has been built to the right of the older one, looking to be from the mid-1800s, and the property's stonewall continues past these for a good distance, once the boundary for pasture lands.

Stonewalls are common in southern New England, most notably in Connecticut and Rhode Island. The Narragansett, the indigenous people that are prominent in Rhode Island continue to be famed stonemasons. More commonly seen are the many dry-stacked stonewalls that follow roadsides and were built by farmers laying out boundaries and, most importantly, keeping livestock contained.

Dairy cows do not like obstacles of any kind, so a low stonewall, say 3 feet high, will keep them securely in pasture. Sheep, however, like goats, are adept climbers, so those old walls you may see that reach 4 or 5 feet high were most likely to keep a flock of sheep, a popular farm animal, both for wool and mutton in eighteenth-century New England.

Another stone wall, a "bank wall" on the crest from the road stands in front of a large white farmhouse that may have its origins in the main house, with extended ells added to its rear. The structure has been modified from what may have been a hall or meetinghouse. Shortly after, another long white picket fence leads past another large house down a long drive and a more modern house close to the road.

Another wooded section follows, where the ridge was blasted to make the road in 1807, the stone abuts the roadside to this day. As you reach West Cornwall, you will notice a handsome Greek Revival home built into the hillside, with a porch that partially extends outward from the hillside, supported by pillars. From here, a cluster of nineteenth-century houses and shops lead into the village.

The old railway station comes into view, and beyond, a former blacksmith and carriage shop that is now a restaurant and the toll house, which dates from the opening of the turnpike in 1809.

The West Cornwall depot was built on the Berkshire branch of the Housatonic Railway between Kent and Caanan, Connecticut. More important perhaps than the people the railway brought to town was the milk train that made regular stops to pick up fresh milk from the nearby farms.

What is now called the West Cornwall covered bridge that crosses the Housatonic River is a wooden-covered lattice trussed bridge that was constructed in its present form around 1864. It was the Hart Bridge in its original form as early as 1762. The Flood of 1837 destroyed the bridge located at this site, and another bridge was completed in 1841. This bridge was also destroyed, leading to the construction of the present bridge, which is unusual in the addition of a second span, as well as queen trusses and supports on the interior.

Drive across the bridge and bear left to take Rt. 7 to Housatonic Meadows or right to head for the border of Massachusetts.

The depot at Sharon, Connecticut, as you enter the village. (*Photo by the author*)

The West Cornwall Covered Bridge (1864) has been restored several times since its completion to maintain its safety, most recently in 2018. It is still open to traffic crossing the Housatonic River. (*Photo by the author*)

9

U.S. ROUTE 7:

SHEFFIELD, MASSACHUSETTS, TO KENT, CONNECTICUT

Begin your journey in Sheffield, Massachusetts, a village nestled in the Housatonic River Valley first settled by a small number of people of European origin who, in the late seventeenth century, had wandered from the Hudson River Valley. A later wave of migration of people from Westfield in the 1720s established a collection of small family farms. The village remained an agricultural community for the next 150 years, with little growth in industry beyond what was needed to sustain the neighboring farms. By 1733, Col. John Ashley had established a grist mill, sawmill, fulling, and cider mills, as well as an iron forge along the dammed Konkapot brook, along a section that would be named Ashley Falls. Today the site is marked by a sign at the bridge that crosses the brook. A later forge, called the "Great Barrington forge," was constructed further up the brook, near its source of Three-Mile Pond, which was there called "Iron Works River."

As industry grew, stores and businesses proliferated along the main roads leading in and out of town. By the 1730s, the village lies between what was simply called "The Hartford Road" leading from the southeast into the village and "Old Albany Road" heading northwest from the village. Travel along the roads was scarce, however, as villagers had few livestock, let alone the luxury of a horse for travel. In 1771, there were only 320 horses in use among a population of 1,500. It is said that the carriage and sleighs owned by Capt. Ezra Fellows, one of the wealthiest men in the village, were the only ones in Sheffield during the eighteenth century. Even by 1837, there were but eighteen carriages in the village.

Travel, then, came mostly from out of town. By 1796, a regular stagecoach run was established. Early coaches, however, were hardly improved from an ordinary wagon, usually open to the elements with hand-hewn benches attached to the floor of the wagon for seating. By the 1830s, with carriage factories in Albany, Hartford, and New Haven, spring-suspended carriages began to be employed, as well as closed carriages that seated up to nine passengers.

In his well-written history of Sheffield, local historian James R. Miller recounts the travels of Giles Andrews, a frequent stage passenger from the town to Albany. Andrews' meticulous recordkeeping of expenses shows that he paid the same $2.50 for the nine years that he took the stage between villages.

Around that same period, Eli Ensign opened a tavern and in "on the plain" or the farmlands that lies outside the village center. Located at the point halfway between Albany and Hartford, it served as an inn or "halfway house" for travelers. Subsequent owners Moses Forbes and his partner, Major Goodwin, expanded the business—adding large barns to the rear of the property that housed up to twenty horses—running three stagecoaches daily.

Blacksmith Jonathan Graham took the opportunity to set up shop across from the tavern to provide repairs to carriages and shoe horses in season. As with our automobiles today, horses needed to be shod at regular intervals, and in winter, with the road packed down for sleighs and wagons with runners, a pair of winter shoes was in order.

The blacksmith shop and house Graham built are still to be seen today on 454 Sheffield Plain (Rt. 7). Easily distinguishable from surrounding houses by its small size and central chimney, the house is now privately owned. The remnants of the inn also remain, though much of the original structure was lost to fire. The house is also privately owned, though a remnant of the "turnabout" or loop before the main house still remains.

Other early taverns included one opened on the Egremont Road as early as 1734 by Nathanial Westover. The squat house near the intersection of West Sheffield Road still stands today and is privately owned. As it lies nearby the field where Shay's rebellious militia took part in a pitched battle with government troops on February 24, 1787, it may well be the place where the soldiers downed "a shot of courage" before the fateful encounter. Today a worn, granite monument sits in a field off-road to mark the site.

Another tavern lies on Main Street as early as 1800. Called the Fellow's Tavern originally, it had the advantage of being located near the site of the constructed railway depot when the Berkshire Railroad linked with the Housatonic Railroad and constructed a 23-mile segment of track that stopped at a depot located at present day Depot Square, off Main Street. The first train arrived on September 28, 1842. The tavern subsequently went through several owners and name changes, including the Taghkanic Inn, Miller Hotel, and Conway House, before being demolished in 1936.

Much of the road through town was greatly improved with the Charter of the "Twelfth Massachusetts Turnpike," issued on June 19, 1801. Although it used part of the old road, it also cut new lanes between meadows and fields to shorten the length of the line between Albany and Hartford, extending some 20 miles from the hamlet of East Sheffield to the center of town, and then on to its destination of Egremont. A section of this route can be found on Pike Road before the village center. The road provided an improved link between the Albany Turnpike and the Greenwoods Turnpike to Hartford was to remain the prominent route for nearly fifty years.

Other turnpike routes soon followed, with the building of the Sheffield–Tryingham turnpike in 1804 and the Sheffield–Great Barrington turnpike constructed in 1807. Throughout the history of roadways in the region, the predominant obstacle to travel was the meandering Housatonic River. By 1829, six bridges had been built to span the river at crossings. These early bridges were in need of yearly repair due to ice jams in winter that damaged trestles and floods in spring that could sometimes wipe out a bridge entirely.

By 1837, after numerous costly repairs to these bridges and others in town, a committee was formed to address the problem. The bridge committee chair H. L. Warner concluded in his report that "it is too apparent to every man in town that our system of building bridges across the Housatonic river is wasting the means & producing no permanent advantage to the public." Warner noted: "… there is, at this time, a decided change in the sentiments of the good people of the town in favor of a more thorough, although more expensive of building our bridges provided it be done with a view to secure permanency and durability."

The first covered bridge in Sheffield was thus constructed at the crossing on present-day Maple Avenue. Built by Lucius and Own Cowles of Westfield, Massachusetts, the structure spanned 126 feet across the river, with a 12-foot clearance and was 15 feet wide. As per the committee's instructions, great care was used in building the foundations for the abutments so that the water would not erode or wash away them away. The bridge opened on September 25, 1837 and would last until 1952 when the river was diverted to avoid flooding adjacent lowlands.

A second covered bridge was constructed over the river in 1854 at a long-used site "where the old bridge now known as the Hubbard bridge" was located. This bridge, according to plan, was built closely to the design of the first, spanning 96 feet across the water. The "Old Covered Bridge," as it came to be called, was closed for restorations in 1970, restored and reopened in 1974, and added to the National Historical Register in 1978. Further funds allowed it to be restored again in 1981 and the original structure survived until it was destroyed by fire in 1994.

Such was the loss of this bridge that it was replaced by the town with another covered bridge that remains today. You may reach the "Old Covered bridge" by heading off Rt. 7 on to Covered Bridge Lane. The bridge is now "off-road," so park your car and take time to explore the careful reconstruction of the bridge with its double tresses, vertical paneling, and gabled roof.

Head back into town and seek out the centrally located Sheffield Historical Society. You can park there and wander through the village, or in the church parking lot nearby. It is well worth a walk, given the number of interesting and well-preserved buildings in this section of the village.

The historical society is headquartered in a fine eighteenth-century brick structure known as the Dan Raymond house (1774). The Federal-style house has five-bay windows on the second floor and four below with a central doorway. Covered with a façade of homemade brick, the house was considered extravagant at the time of its construction; however, it soon became known as one of the finest houses on Main Street.

Raymond was a local merchant and loyalist, even as the fervor of support for the patriot cause grew swiftly in the town. Sheffield had voted early on to support a boycott of British goods, and men from the town had been involved in an organized "shutdown" of adjacent Great Barrington in 1774, considered one of the first acts of rebellion in the region. On June 18, 1776, the town voted in support on independence from the mother country, and on the day that the Declaration of Independence was signed, the town planted a "liberty tree" in town. The tree, however, was cut down sometime during the evening after its dedication.

The perpetrator turned out to be Dan Raymond and his servant. After being convicted of the act, Raymond was forced to walk through a gauntlet of the men in town, apologizing to each one. His servant was tarred and feathered, and also made to present himself at the doors of local prominent patriots and apologize in turn. The house is open for tours in season and furnished with furniture and artifacts from the period. On the extensive property are also several historic buildings preserved by the historical society.

An 1870s two-story barn holds an impressive collection of tools and farm equipment from the era. An 1876 "growing house" served as an indoor garden for fresh green throughout the year; it is now used as an Education Center. A small law office constructed about 1820 for attorney Parker Hall and his associates was originally on the "Sheffield Plain" before being rescued from demolition by the society and moved to its present location in 1970.

The property also holds a rare double chamber smokehouse designed by Edward Fellows Ensign in 1838 is also on the property. It was moved to the grounds and restored by the historical society in 2000, and once supplied the needs of the Ensign family, as well the "Old Stone Store" adjacent to the society's headquarters.

Major Eli Ensign constructed the impressive Greek revival mercantile building in 1834 with stone from a local quarry. It was acquired by the town

The Dan Raymond House (1774). Raymond was a merchant and loyalist who stirred controversy in the town. His former grand home is now occupied by the Sheffield Historical Society. (*Photo by the author*)

Maj. Eli Ensigns mercantile building (1840), now known as the "old stone store." (*Photo by the author*)

in 1878 and used as the town hall until a new building was constructed just behind the original store. It is now among the properties held by the historical society and used as a gift shop and exhibit space.

Next door to the Old Stone Store is the Old Parish Church, constructed in 1760 after the congregation outgrew its original building, which had been erected on the Sheffield Plain in 1735. The church also functioned as the town meeting house. It was moved to its present location in 1819, when the present steeple and bell were added to the original structure. It was then renamed the First Congregational Church of Sheffield. A second, simpler structure that resembles a meetinghouse or early church is just a short distance away, off Rt. 7 at the intersection of Root Lane.

I would encourage visitors to walk the approximately half mile from Root Lane north along Rt. 7, going back towards the historical society and beyond to view the well-preserved eighteenth- and nineteenth-century houses that make up the Sheffield Historic District. A few examples of what you will find are here.

Across Rt. 7 is the Samuel Herrup Antique Shop. You will notice the twin gabled roofs and may wonder how the structure came to be that way. The house was conjoined in the twentieth century, with the left side being built in the nineteenth century and serving as the post office until 1952. Its tin ceiling is a remnant of that period. The structure has been an elegant, high-quality antique shop since 1971. The owner, Samuel Herrup, is a descendant of Jonathan Herrup, the first minister in Sheffield, and his family lives a short distance away in the home that was built as his parish house.

Walking past the historical society, you will find on the left, a structure that resembles a small house. This is an eighteenth-century hatter's shop, also rescued by the historical society. Mark Dewey built his "hat factory" in 1816, when he lived in the Dan Raymond house. An advertisement for the December 5, 1816 edition of the *Berkshire Star* promises the proprietor "… has now, and will constantly keep on hand, a handsome assortment of Hats."

Just a few steps away, you will find another impressive stone structure. This is the Owen Dewey Hall (1887). The hall was designed by Boston architect William Ralph Emerson and built with local stone from the Taconic range and blue dolomite from a local farm.

Owen Dewey was born in Sheffield in 1794. He spent his formative years in the town on his family's farm and attended school in Sheffield. According to biographer Caroline Miller, his mother's piety heavily influenced him, and his love of learning came from years of reading by torchlight in the town library, whose 200 books were considered a treasure by the young scholar.

He attended Williams College and returned to Sheffield as an apprentice in Charles Dewey's law practice. Illness and a period of introspection drew him away from the law toward theology, but he taught school in town and

The castle-like Owen Dewey Hall (1887) designed by Boston architect William Ralph Emerson. (*Photo by the author*)

then worked in a dry goods store in New York before he entered Andover Theological School. He soon found himself troubled by the Calvinistic doctrines that colored his studies and left Andover in 1819 to spent eight months working with the American Education Society.

Shortly after, Dewey was invited to spend a year as pastor of a small Congregational Church in Gloucester, Massachusetts, and embraced Unitarianism, a theology more suited to his personal beliefs and empathy for people of all races and backgrounds—an "open and caring support for all in the community."

The decision outraged his fellow parishioners at the Sheffield Congregationalist Church, which refused to allow him to attend services. He would not enter his home church again until he was allowed to give a lecture on its Centennial in 1876 when he was eighty-two years of age.

He spent a remarkable career in the pulpit, assigned to churches in New Bedford, Massachusetts, New York, and Washington. He returned to Sheffield after his retirement in 1849. He settled down with his family and lived modestly, writing lectures that he would later be invited to deliver at the Lowell Institute and similar establishments around the country.

Dewey traveled to Charleston, South Carolina, in the winter of 1856–57, and while preaching there, he became troubled by "the ground recently taken at the South—that the institute of slavery is intrinsically right, just and good—

seems to me to involve such a wrong in humanity, such evil to the South and such peril to the Union of the States…"

He returned to Sheffield and began to give abolitionist talks under "the Big Elm" the following summer as Congress continued to debate the issue. Dewey considered the question of permitting slavery "the great trial question of the country."

The long-time minister retired permanently to Sheffield in 1861, engaging himself in local causes, especially in the founding of the Sheffield Friendly Union Library Association, founded in 1871 "to increase good and kindly feelings and to promote intelligence and good thinking." The Association met one evening a week during the winter for the purpose of "social entertainment and culture," to "enjoy music, lectures, reading, dramas, or whatever diversion its managers can procure." Dewey himself gave several talks on Shakespeare before his death in 1882 just a week shy of his eighty-eighth birthday.

The hall we see today was erected by friends in his memory and serves the purpose laid out by Dewey himself in its founding years, offering music, plays, and other cultural entertainment throughout the year.

Once you have taken in the Sheffield Historical District, a short car drive away will take you to another historic site worth visiting before you begin your journey farther south into Connecticut.

The handsome Asley House and adjacent farm and forest were the home of John Ashley, the largest landowner in Sheffield. Historian James Miller writes: "In 1771 the largest farm had 50 cultivated acres. It was a property of Juhn Ashley, who employed three teams each of oxen and horses in its operation, animals in numbers no other farmer in town could claim to own."

Col. John Ashley, as he was called after the Revolutionary War, had built the house in 1735 after marriage to his Dutch wife, Hanna Hogeboom. He accumulated land over the years and became deeply involved in the town's patriot activities, heading the committee that penned the *Sheffield Resolves* in 1773—an early petition against British tyranny.

As you head south on Rt. 7, you may notice signs that name the route the "Elizabeth Freeman Highway." Freeman was a slave on Ashley's farm with five others. Known in her old age as "Mum Bett," there were rumors that she was Ashley's daughter, but she remained silent on the issue. She won her freedom in a lawsuit against Ashley in 1781, inspired, it has been written, by the Revolutionary War and its declaration for equality for all.

To visit the historic house and its fine collections, bear right on to Rt. 7A or Ashley Falls Road and continue until another right will bring you on to Rannapo Rd. Continue for some distance until another right on to Cooper Hill Road. (If you cross Stony Brook, you have missed the turn.) The house museum is easily found and has ample parking. Tours will take an hour, and if you want to hike in the woods known as Bartholomew's Cobble, the full 5 miles will take another two hours. Be sure to bring decent hiking boots for the rocky trails. You may also want to visit nearby Mount Washington Everett State Park

Getting back on to Rt. 7 South, you may return to Rannapo Road and continue on it east to Ashley Falls road. Taking a right will bring you back to Rt. 7 just above Barracks Road. Be mindful of the signs as you head south, especially at the intersection of Rt. 44. Rt. 7 South will briefly join with Rt. 44 East before turning off again on its own. This small stretch of roadway must have been bustling at one time as it led goods and passengers to and from the intersection of two ancient roadways.

Continuing on Rt. 7 South, you have the option of visiting yet another impressive bridge above an even more impressive waterfall in Falls Village. Look for Rt. 126 West and take the short ride into this pleasant village.

Falls Village was once called Canaan Falls and was later part of Amesville. During the time of both the Revolutionary War and the Civil War, factories here were an important supplier of armaments to the Continental and Union Armies. As you enter into town, look for Railroad Street, then bear left onto Water Street as it dips below the railroad bridge and leads past a hydroelectric power plant on the left and to a parking lot further along. A newly installed gravel path has been made up to viewing points of the falls along the Housatonic river.

An alternative path, which I took myself, would be to park in town, pay a visit to the Historical Society, and then take the small stretch of the Appalachian Trail from the end of which leads to the Iron bridge above the Great Falls.

In 1734, early settlers of the town parceled the piece of land along the river and "ye Grate Falls" to Humphrey Avery, provided that he build a sawmill before the end of that year. The power from the falls allowed the construction of fulling mills for the sheared wool of the village sheep, gristmills, blacksmith shops, and then iron mills all proliferated along the river. A bridge was built over the river at this site as early as 1744.

In 1833, the Ames Iron Works opened on the Salisbury side of the river. In its first years of production, workers manufactured axles and wheels for locomotives, steamboat shafts, and anchors. By the time of the Civil War, the iron works employed hundreds of workers who made cannon and cannon balls for the Union Army.

In 1845, a plan was forwarded to create a three-level, mile-long canal to power the industry below the falls. The canal was created but failed to make any improvement to local industry. The remains of the canal are still visible, and that of the iron works are all that remain of the village's most active period.

When the Housatonic Railway came to Caanan Falls in 1841, it named the station "Falls Village," and the town adapted that name shortly after.

Great Falls, in the village of Falls Village, Connecticut. (*Photo by the author*)

When you are ready to resume your journey along Rt. 7 South, simply retrace your route back to Rt. 126 East and then to Rt. 7 South again.

Shortly after you return to Rt. 7 South, you will enter the town of Sharon, Connecticut, which holds the Housatonic Meadows State Forest and the Housatonic Meadows campground, which will appear on the left side of the road.

Having stayed at the campground during each of my visits to this region, I highly recommend it. There are clean showers and bathrooms available, as well as dumpsters for removing debris from your campsite (important in an area frequented during the spring and early summer by black bears).

Some ninety-five sites are scattered on its grounds, the most coveted being those on the river. On the north side of the campground lies a number of sites that allow direct access to the river, which, here, is quiet and often shallow after the spring season. Some enterprising campers have built small stone dams in places to create bathing pools.

Several cabins have also been built on sites with river access, and above, the sites are perched on a hillside above a stretch that contains some class II rapids in good season. For myself, few experiences can match falling asleep in a tent to the sound of a passing river.

A word of friendly caution about the river: as a long-time kayaker, I know to secure a map and, if available, some in-person discussion about any river

A view of the Housatonic River as seen from Housatonic Meadows State Park and campground. (*Photo by the author*)

before I put into the water. The Housatonic has some beautiful stretches of quiet water for lazy paddling and bird watching, but other places are very shallow and often require you to pull your kayak or canoe through considerable stretches of the river. It can also abruptly enter a stronger current and quickly churn through a stretch of boulder-strewn bedrock, becoming class II rapids, before settling into quiet water once again downstream.

If you plan ahead of time, you might join a friendly group from the Sheffield Congregational Church, which meets regularly to paddle on the river, or find another group with an experienced guide to make your experience a memorable and safe outing.

If a decent hike is part of your itinerary, there is access to the nearby Appalachian Trail from two nearby trails. One is a steep ascent that begins from a field across from the Housatonic Meadows Campground, with another just down Rt. 7 on the right-hand side of the road just before the intersection with Rt. 4.

There, at the trailhead of the Mohawk Trail, you will find a small parking area and trail map. This easy ascent leads to part of the Appalachian Trail and will allow you to do a loop around the ridge of the Lime-Rock section of the Housatonic State Forest. Be sure to take a map from the trailhead pavilion or study the large map posted on the board before heading out so that you do not meander on the Appalachian Trail off the loop.

This part of the AT, though in a lower altitude, still has some fine views and overlooks. I had done a good portion of the AT when I was twenty-four years old and was thrilled to recognize an overlook I had first seen some thirty-three years before when I first walked the loop several years ago.

Returning to Rt. 7 South, as you approach the intersection of Rt. 4, you may not be aware that you are traveling on a true engineering marvel. The Cornwall Bridge, as it is known, was built in 1930 by the firm of C. W. Blakeslee & Sons and is the largest concrete open spandrel-designed bridge in the region.

Spanning 674 feet across the Housatonic River and the adjacent railway bed of the Housatonic River Railway, the bridges six open-spandrel arches carries two lanes of traffic from the southern end of Sharon Connecticut into the small village of Cornwall Bridge, so named because a bridge was constructed here early on, with the present bridge replacing a nineteenth-century covered bridge.

The present bridge was renovated in 1994 and placed on the National Register of Historic Places in 2004. To truly appreciate the engineering of this bridge, take a left on to Rt. 4, park along the curb, and get a full look at the spanned arches underneath the roadway.

As you re-enter Rt. 7 South, be mindful of the three-way intersection that leads in and out of Cornwall Bridge. The market on the left is a good place to purchase any camping or travel items you may need, as well as getting a bite to eat. Sandwiches are made by hand at the deli, and ready-to-go meals are also available along with homemade muffins and pastries.

Continue your drive south and you will soon come upon the Kent Falls State Park. This will be on the left-hand side of the road, and there is ample parking just off the road. The park is a popular place to picnic with its sprawling, open grounds, and the quiet flow of Falls Brook beyond the main attraction of Kent Falls.

The source of the falls is Falls Brook, which flows west from the town of Warren and plunges in a 70-foot cascade over the limestone face of the cliff, which then separates into a series of lesser falls that spray over the visitors who climb on the rock ledge below. The brook continues through a section of the park, where it pools into bathing areas for children and meanders quietly through. Beyond the park, Falls Brook descends another 200 feet into the valley and enters the Housatonic river a quarter-mile away.

Most visitors are content to sunbathe on the warm ledge that lies along the brook and take in the magnificence of this display of nature. There is more to be seen on short walking trails to the top of the falls and a small covered bridge near the parking area, which is a favorite photo opportunity for visitors.

Kent Falls Park began with the gift of 200 acres in 1919 from the White Memorial Foundation. Other donations allowed for the further purchase of adjoining acreage, and at present the park has some 295 acres. The park grounds were developed during the W.P.A. era, and the Youth Conservation Corps cut the trails used by visitors in the 1970s. A dedicated park employee named Edmund Palmer built the authentic reproduction of a covered bridge on the site in 1994. The park is a perfect stop for a picnic, or those sandwiches bought at the market back in Cornwall Bridge. As with any state park in Connecticut, you are not allowed to bring alcohol on the premises, and please place any trash in the containers at the parking lot before you leave.

Continuing south, you will soon notice a cluster of museums, including the Eric Sloane museum. When I came across the museum some years ago by accident, it was one of those serendipitous moments that erase whatever lingering doubt you may have held against taking an unknown road, going off the planned route you had carefully mapped, and stepping outside, as they say now, "your comfort zone."

Illustrator and author Eric Sloane (1905–1985) has been a favorite of mine since I was a teenager, poring through his books illustrated with old barns and outbuildings, and with explanations on how they were constructed. Sloane also authored and illustrated a book on the astonishing number and variety of tools used in carpentry and on the average farm. *A Reverence for Wood*, *A Museum of Early American Tools*, and *Diary of an Early American Boy: Noah Blake 1805* were among my early favorite books.

Sloane's work today is known for its authenticity and for being the authority on early American architecture and tool making. His work is a frequent reference for me today as I volunteer at Smith's Castle, near Wickford, Rhode Island. Attics and cellars in two houses on the property have yielded an assortment of tools and pieces of tools or machinery over the years, most of which have been identified and archived, but there remain a few mysteries.

Visitors may see a replica of the cabin he built for his studio, and a modern building that houses a collection of original painting and drawings, as well as Sloane's private collection of the tools he illustrated for his books, donated to the state of Connecticut by the Stanley Works tool making company in 1969.

The collection is impressive and thoughtfully displayed for visitors to obtain an understanding as Sloane tried to convey in his books of how the craft of woodworking evolved and what is lost to us now, as machines have taken over what were once hand wrought detail. Today, almost every piece of trim, cornices, clapboards, and shingle can easily be picked up, cheaply made, and cheaply priced at one of the do-it-yourself outlets in your nearby roadside mall.

The adjacent gallery gives us an inside view to Sloane's ideas and the evolution of his own painting and drawing over the years, including those of clouds for his books on weather and storms. It was also interesting to learn that while he painted barns for a living as a young man, it was not until the

The Eric Sloane Museum, Rt. 7, Kent, Connecticut. (*Photo by the author*)

Sloane's cabin where he worked on his paintings and illustrations. (*Photo by the author*)

1950s—when he purchased and began to renovate an early farm—that his interest in researching and illustrating that subject began.

All the more impressive then are his achievements in presenting early America so well, as well as books on weather and astronomy that are now considered classics in their field as well.

The museum was built on the grounds of the Kent Furnace, the remains of its massive oven built into the hillside may be seen, The giant kiln for pig iron was built in 1826, designed so that men could roll wheelbarrows of iron ore to the top of the furnace and continually fuel the oven during the course of the day's production. The iron works at the site continued for some seventy years.

A section of the Housatonic River slips by the property here, and a footpath along the riverbank is illustrated by informative signs on the iron production that occurred on the site. Adjacent to the museum is also the Connecticut Antique Machinery Museum. The museum holds a section of railway a pair of steam powered locomotives and a few railcars associated with the ironworks, as well as a large building of tractors and farm machinery.

Stopping for a couple of hours at this site gives you an impressive display of early American craftsmanship and industry that was an integral part of this community, and many others along the Housatonic River.

The massive Kent Furnace, built into the side of a hill, so that a road on the ridge could be constructed for men to push wheelbarrows of wood for fuel to the top of the furnace.

10

THE OLD HOMESTEAD HIGHWAY:

WORCESTER, MASSACHUSETTS, TO KEENE, NEW HAMPSHIRE

Worcester is a city that I will always remember as the place where my parents, returning from our yearly visits to Vermont, would inevitably get lost. So numerous are the route twists and turns through the city that only recently have improvements been made via the highway to get in and out of certain sections of the city with ease.

And so I apologize to the reader and potential traveler for starting one of these journeys here. But as with many other New England communities, Worcester, Massachusetts, was a hub of industry and freight exchange throughout the years of stagecoach travel. Bear with the traffic as you head along 122N.

Buildings that had much to do with the city's history remain, from the meat-packing plant to the Table Talk Pie Bakery, which still bear the painted signs on their brick walls. Blocks of the old city, long neglected, will eventually give way to a pleasant drive through an early suburb still within its boundaries, and becomes a quiet country road as we head into Paxton.

The town boasts two expansive wooded parks within its boundaries. A short drive on Mower Lane off 122N will bring you to the Brayton Parkway and the Cascades West Conservation area, a large protected woodland that stretches east to Silver Brook and the Holden Reservoir.

The Cascades holds over 156 acres that has been protected by the Worcester Land Trust since 1991. A trail system leads visitors to Cascade Falls, and into the adjacent Cascade and Boynton Parks. If you choose to have a picnic or take a hike, simply follow Brayton Pkwy back to Mower Street, take a right and follow Mower to the end of Camp Street to 122N.

Continuing on 122N, you pass a farm and garden shop and soon will see signs on the left for the Muir Meadows Conservation area. This 57-acre parcel of woodland is also managed by the Worcester Land Trust and has an extensive trail system leading through the expansive meadows to Southwick Pond in the neighboring town of Leicester, Massachusetts.

Parking is available in a small lot across the brook at the corner of 122N and Indian Hill Road. An alternative area closer to the pond can be found at the end of Walbridge Street; take a left a little further up the road. You soon enter the center of Paxton. Granted its charter in 1765 to become a district of Worcester County, the town likely had less than 300 inhabitants at its beginnings. By 1790, there were 558; the population in the nineteenth century rising to a peak of 850 inhabitants, before steadily declining as the century closed. Once the town held a thriving shoe and boot-making industry, but by the end of the nineteenth century, it was purely an agrarian community.

In the spring of 1766, the citizens voted in a town meeting to contribute 250 pounds towards the "building of a meeting- house and meeting-house place." The completed building included a "negro seats in the rear of the front gallery," "for slaves of the congregation," and "the old people's in front of the pulpit, for the use of the deaf." Today, as you enter the old town center, a large white building that resembles a church comes into view. The town's nineteenth-century town hall was originally located in the basement of what was then the First Congregational Church. It was moved from the "common" across the street in 1824 and rededicated at its present location in 1836 at the intersection of Routes 31 and 122.

A small common with a memorial remains on the left, the whole divided by the construction of Rt. 31. Beyond the intersection, the old common continues, a granite obelisk to commemorate the town's civil war dead at its center. The large three-story rectangular-shaped town hall was constructed in an economic "stick-style" with overhanging eaves, and the whole originally ornamented with decorative gable trusses and window brackets. Narrow four-over four-paned windows line the façade in perfect alignment with the columned and balconied entryway. A gable truss was included on the front of the building with a stained-glass window installed behind the truss. Most of these ornamental additions were later removed. The resulting changes left the building as a plain, colonial-like structure, and as such, it was painted white and fitted with black shutters.

Today, the shutters have been removed and the town hall is the subject of a major restoration project, hoping to turn the nineteenth-century behemoth built by Simon Allen into a twenty-first-century office building.

While the building was constructed in a simple Agrarian design outside, the exterior belays the elegant detail inside with its massive hall and balcony.

The town of Paxton lost an iconic building adjacent to the town hall when the historic Paxton Inn burned to the ground in 2001. Constructed by Jobiah Clark in 1759, the inn was a regular stop on the Barre–Paxton–Worcester stagecoach line and a vacation destination by the twentieth century. The inn and town hall were both featured on numerous postcards in the late nineteenth and early twentieth century.

An iconic restaurant nearby was the "Brick Steamer," which was the old restaurant at the Paxton Navy Yard, constructed originally from a landlocked tugboat. Later construction made the restaurant a tourist destination, serving lunch, dinner, and ice cream to passing motorists.

Just past this intersection, Massachusetts state highway 56 aligns with Rt. 122N. Look for a brightly painted red mill building on the right. This likely dates from the early nineteenth century, though it has been greatly modified.

Farther along on the left, a large colonial house looms with its piedmont doorway and a total of eleven windows spread about its façade. This is the fourth oldest house in Paxton, constructed between 1729 and 1743 by Moses Parkinhurst. A later addition on the left side of the house seems to have added an additional four windows to the original structure. The front of the house is bordered by a simple but elegant wooden fence and a long stonewall that extends to the end of the property line.

Another large nineteenth-century house, pieced together from two separate houses, lies just beyond. The original house holds a large Federal-style doorway at its corner with a sunken entryway and sidelights whose panes extend nearly the length of the door.

Continuing on Rt. 122N, we leave the remains of historic Paxton behind and for the next several miles drive past more modern commercial buildings and housing before the road again resumes as a quiet country lane between woods and farmland.

As you bear left at Turkey Hill Rd to continue on Rt. 122, you are now entering the old Barre–Paxton road. Traveling through the heavily wooded, sparsely housed region, you will notice small parking areas for trailheads on both sides of the road. To visit Rutland State Park, take a right on North Brookfield Road and another right on to Whitehall Road and follow through until you see signs for parking.

The woodlands are largely uninterrupted until you reach a long body of water called Powder Mill Pond and the Ware River. Continue on 122N and just past the intersections of Town Farm Road and Fruitland Road, you will enter a congested area. Rt. 32 South appears on the left, but continue on Rt. 122N and as Barre Road ends and Summer Street begins, Rt. 32N aligns with Rt. 122N into the old historic district of Barre.

A handsome common, with a classic white New England gazebo, is on the left. The elegant Greek Revival house beyond the commons is now the home of the Barre Historical Society. On the right, a few older buildings remain, but as with the town of Paxton, Barre suffered the loss of its most iconic building to fire.

Postcard of "The Brick Steamer" restaurant in Paxton, Massachusetts (*c.* 1920s). (*Author's collection*)

Postcard of the Hotel Barre (*c.* 1920s). (*Author's collection*)

The Hotel Barre was opened on June 12, 1889 to much fanfare and a brass band that serenaded some 250 dinner guests at $1 per plate. The hotel, which was the third establishment to be built on the commons, was to outdo the other local hostelries by its grandeur alone.

The structure rose three stories above its entryway, with columned balconies that extended on each side and above the entry, topped by an octagonal cupola. As written in an article by Lester W. Paquin on the Barre Historical Society's blog, the interior of the Hotel Barre "...was a symphony of richly toned woodwork and crystal, with all of the most modern conveniences-hot and cold running water, indoor 'facilities', gas lighting and steam heat."

Such a grand structure required much maintenance, and with poor bookings by 1895, the hotel could no longer sustain itself and the company that had built the hotel went into receivership. An original investor took possession of the property, but by 1889, it had transferred the deed to the Barre Village Improvement Society. The society kept the hotel opened for a time, but as with the original owners, the expense of maintaining such a structure became overwhelming.

The BVIS sold the hotel to George Prouty after 1899, and the hotel continued to operate, but in a steady state of decline. By the time of Mr. Prouty's death in 1934, only two tenants lived inside the building.

Several owners would then invest in the building over the coming years, a brief scare occurring in 1941 when the owner threatened to tear the hotel down over the refusal of a liquor license from town selectmen. In the end, an agreement was reached and the hotel remained on the commons.

Between 1942 and 1960, a series of what were to become iconic murals were painted in the public rooms of the hotel by the Matello's, a father and son team from Connecticut. One of these now privately-owned murals was part of an exhibition on the anniversary of the hotel's opening in 2015.

By 1965, the hotel once again had new owners. Linda and Edward Mansueti operated the establishment as the Barre Guest House and opened a popular bar in the basement called the "Hunt Club" on the Grove Street side of the building. The couple owned the hotel until 1981, when a series of attempts to sell the hotel fell through until a new partnership named MRW Inc. took possession of the property.

The new investors spared no expense in restoring the hotel to its former glory:

> The broad piazza now featured a long row of green "Kennedy" rockers for those inclined to take their ease on Barre Common. The public rooms on the first floor were now furnished with exquisite antiques and important works of art and sculpture. Woodwork gleamed as new, draperies gathered and puddle in

abundant excess, oriental carpets once again provided comfort beneath, grand staircases became art galleries, and restored period lighting fixtures illuminated it all...

The Hunt Club was moved to the main floor as a "gentleman's bar" and the old bar was renamed the "Side-Door Saloon." An octagonal suite was installed inside the old tower, and the culmination of the elegant restoration was best seen in the silver and white themed "Cotillion Room," which featured a crystal-swagged chandelier that nearly spanned the length of the ceiling. It also featured two large colonial portraits of an early Rhode Island governor and his wife, reportedly purchased at auction from the Rhode Island state house.

The restored grandeur of the old hotel was celebrated by the town on the 100th anniversary of its opening, with hundreds attending the celebration on the common, taking tours of the hotel. In the evening, an invitation-only champagne reception toasted the return of the Hotel Barre's fortunes.

As it turns out, those fortunes had been steadily declining. Just months before the celebration, MRW Inc. had filed for Chapter 11 bankruptcy. On August 27, 1990, the company was declared insolvent by a federal magistrate and the doors of the grand hotel were closed.

Just two days later, a neighbor spied smoke coming from the hotel windows in late afternoon. The resulting fire destroyed the entire structure, leaving only a portion of the façade standing amid the ruins.

There is little doubt that a structure of its grandeur will not be seen again in Barre, but today, the charm of the village is in those well preserved houses that do remain and perhaps stand out all the more for the lack of a wedding-cake hotel in the center of the historic district.

To resume your journey, continue straight on Rt. 32/122 North. You will notice an impressive brick library on the left, and to the right, an expansive memorial park has several monuments on its grounds. The white spire of the Barre Congregational church towers above the trees at the northern end of the park.

The road curves left at a cozy inn, and continues past an array of nineteenth-century houses and the old high school. Soon, the houses thin out again, and the road becomes bordered by woods and farmland once again. An impressive farm soon comes into view beyond long pastures on either side, and the farm, with its large nineteenth-century farmhouse and outgrowth of whitewashed barns and outbuildings, also holds a large farm stand for travelers.

Continuing on Rt. 32/122N past more pasturelands we soon find another farm with its nineteenth-century farmhouse made of two conjoined houses across from a large, weathered barn.

The Stone Cow Brewery, BBQ, and ice-cream stand. (*Photo by the author*)

Just ahead, you will notice a stone cow on the right-hand side of the road. This is the Stone Cow Brewery and BBQ. The brewery is the latest venture for the Stevens family that maintains the Carter-Stevens Farm, a dairy concern that has operated since 1938. The original farm dates back to 1700, and the barn that serves as the main building of the business dates back to at least 1820.

The family opened an ice-cream stand about fifteen years ago, but faced with the challenges that confront any modern dairy, Sean Dubois and his wife, Molly, who grew up on the farm, began the brewery and BBQ, which soon became a popular destination for daytrips from Worcester or Springfield. The taproom routinely offers a choice of ten beers brewed on the property, and the BBQ features wood-grilled burgers and smoked brisket from grass-fed cattle. Picnic tables out front and a back patio offer plenty of room (and great views) for eating your meal.

On a warm summer day, the hazy Bono Loco IPA with its citrus-flavored hops is a great accompaniment to your lunch or dinner. The hand-crafted brews like Bono-Loco IPA, Cows Out Milk Stout, Farmhouse Ale, and others have become popular staples at local liquor stores as well.

Resuming our drive along 122/32N, we roll past more farms and woodlands. The two-lane country road continues, the woodlands interspersed here and there with houses and small businesses. Just past Pat Conner Road you will enter the Swift River Preserve, and as you cross a section of an old cement bridge, you will notice a waterfall on your right, and beyond, Connor's Pond, which the road follows as you continue north. The large body of water is fed by both the East Branch of the Swift River and Rutland Brook.

Continue along Rt. 122/32N into the town of Petersham. Within a short drive, you will enter a more populated area. Look for an impressive old farmhouse on the left and its stonewalls that line the roadside. As you reach a series of small businesses and Quabbin Woods, look for another old farm on the left, with a fine stone barn before the large farmhouse. Just ahead is the intersection where Rt. 32N turns right and Rt. 122 continues straight. Slow down and turn right to follow 32N where you enter one of the most picturesque stretches of the road.

Nineteenth-century houses line the road and, on the right, an expansive stonewall borders the fields adjacent to an old farm and another stone barn.

As you continue, more modern houses appear, but then give way to the heart of Petersham with its small brick town clerk's office, an imposing town hall, built as a twentieth-century reproduction on the site of the original meeting house, and large country store (1842), all facing the common. Most of the buildings situated around the area of the common were constructed before 1850. The town was incorporated in 1754 and was the scene of the second battle of Shays' Rebellion in 1787. Just beyond the common is the town's historical society library, originally built as a schoolhouse in 1848.

An old stonewall borders a field in Petersham, New Hampshire.

In the blink of an eye, the road again becomes a country lane. A few Greek Revival, Federal, and Victorian houses lead from the center of town, and an old church lies across from the historic law office of Aaron Brooks and the North Common Meadow, a 25-acre preserve that offers short trails around the meadow and pond, as well as a spur trail into the nearby Brooks Woodland Preserve and Roaring Brook.

The road continues along through a populated area and then thins out again to woodlands and pastures. As you approach the intersection of Rt. 101, look for a red barn adjacent to another large eighteenth-century farmhouse and outbuildings bordered by a white wooden fence. Within a few miles, shortly after passing Pierce Road on the right, look for the sign directing you to the Fisher Museum of the Harvard Forest off Prospect Hill Road.

The 4,000-acre Harvard Forest was first established in 1907 as a conservation area and has been a long-term research and educational site since 1988. The museum displays some twenty-three dioramas of the history, conservation, and management of the forests in central New England.

Outside, self-guided natural history and ecology trails offer easy hiking, with the longest trail a moderate 2.5-mile walk through the forest. A field guide to the plants of Harvard Forest is available in the museum, and limited guided tours of the trails are also offered. Be aware, that as with other locations of the Harvard Forest, hunting is permitted in season.

Continue on Rt. 32N through several more miles of thickly forested roadside. In time, you will drive under the overpass of Rt. 202, and then as you approach the town of Athol, the road merges with Rt. 2A. Little remains of historical significance in Athol, though there are some well-preserved nineteenth-century houses along Main Street. A plaque marks the site of an old tollgate and the historical society resides in a nicely restored church just before you reach the intersection, where Rt. 2A/32N bears right off of School Street.

Shortly after this intersection, Rt. 2A continues straight while Rt. 32 bears right at Chestnut Hill Ave. A steel bridge carries you across Miller's River. Continue past the old mill buildings on the left, cross another bridge (with a paved surface), and then take a left to continue on Rt. 32N. Bear right again as the road merges with Crescent Street, and then take another right to continue on to Rt. 32N at Silver Lake Street (the Athol Mini-Mart is on the right).

Drive on past more houses and extended farmlands, bearing left when you reach Royalston Road to continue on Rt. 32N. The road travel's once again through farmlands and some heavily wooded areas as you reach West Royalston, and eventually the Tully Dam on the right side of the road.

Constructed in 1949 by the Army Corp of Engineers, the resultant Tully Lake is a 1,262-acre reservoir that prevents flooding from Millers River and the Connecticut River. The dam has a capacity to hold over 6 billion gallons of water and can contain over 7 inches of rain runoff and has a downstream channel

Tully Dam and reservoir, constructed to relieve the flooding of towns from Miller's and the Connecticut River in 1949. (*Photo by the author*)

capacity of 850 cubic feet per second. An estimate by the USACE in 2007, determined that the dam had prevented $26 million dollars in flood damages.

The dam and lake have always been a memorable stopping place when our family traveled along this route to Keene, New Hampshire. It is both an engineering marvel and a place of stunning beauty. Take the time to cross the road and take in the view of the east branch of Tully river as it winds through the valley.

Continuing on Rt. 32N, we enter a long stretch of road long remembered in our family as a twisting, turning rollercoaster ride through the woodlands. Indeed, our father seemed to delight in speeding along this well-known route, much to the consternation of our mother and the delight of us children.

Driving the route today, the hills and twists and turns seem to carry on for miles though the element of surprise and delight is still there as, after a mile of heavily shaded road, a curtain is lifted and the sunlight appears through open fields and a brightly painted barn and farmhouse.

Though a white farmhouse is still the prevailing color in New England today, traveling along this route you will find bright yellow farmhouses, even barns the same cheerful color; though most are painted in the red that we have come to associate with barns. But even more so are those that remain unpainted. These are not necessarily unused or neglected buildings, but the long-standing rule that a man who owned a farm was judged by the condition of his barn even more than his house, has long fallen by the wayside.

As you travel, be mindful of Rt. 68 (Warwick Road) merging on to the road from the right and then quickly veering off to the left. Otherwise, the route is an unimpeded chute through sparsely populated areas. These woodlands are part of the Royalston Town Forest. Keep an eye out for the trailhead to Royalston Falls on the right. As you reach Bliss Hill Road on the left, you will enter the town of Richmond in the state of New Hampshire.

You quickly pass through a cluster of rural homesteads and continue along what is now the Athol Road and come to the intersection of Rt. 119. A small shopping area gives us the opportunity to park and take note of the remaining common and small park at the intersection.

The site is where the town common once stood and held a watering trough and pump for travelers, and the town well. There was a sign as well, directing travelers to destinations in each direction, and in 1855, the town decorated the common with a stone wheel from the original town grist mill.

The great white house lying at the east of the intersection, and across from the park, was constructed in 1798 and was known as the Widow Howe's Tavern. The small park that graces the intersection is named for Geraldine Brewer, the town's unofficial greeter in her capacity, who was working at the 4 Corners Store that long stood at the intersection for forty-eight years. The original store, according to an early local history of the town, was built by Maj. James Robinson in 1815 to accommodate travelers on the newly constructed Ashuelot turnpike. She did not have far to travel to work, for she lived in the house once owned by widow Howe.

From here, the road becomes what remains of the Old Homestead Highway. Originally laid out in 1765–1766, the road was greatly improved in 1770, running north for roughly 4½ miles until it intersected with another road that had been laid out to Swanzy. The entire roadway was relaid in 1784 and became the route for mail delivery from Worcester to Keene. The first carrier was Jonathan Pierce a reputedly large, jovial man from Royalston, who trod the route in a one-horse shay for twenty years. By 1830, the mail was later carried by stagecoaches run by Jonas Foristall and Russell Wheeler. A later carrier was Bennoi Ballou of Richmond, who used a horse and wagon to take on packages as well for "express delivery."

Other stages traveled the run daily on business for many years until the coming of the railroad line to Fitchburg. By 1876, only one stage remained traveling the old highway three days a week. Traveling through Richmond, one is always in the shadow of Mount Monadnock, the state's most visited mountain despite those bumper stickers you see about Mt. Washington.

Mount Monadnock rises 3,165 feet above the surrounding woodlands. The myriad of well-traveled trails that lead to the summit are easy to moderately graded. As teenagers and young adults when we came to the mountain, we would try to be the fastest climber to the top, and then run back down through the wooded trails to be the first to the bottom. This was no easy task, as there was often company on the trails in young hikers or older adults, annoyed as we squeezed past them on the trail as they stopped to catch their breath.

Monadnock is said to be the second most visited mountain in the world, after Mount Fuji in Japan. As you travel through the town and on to Swanzy, you may catch glimpses of the mountain to the east, rising in a gentle wave to its bald peak.

As you come closer to Keene, look for the sign on the right that leads you to a classic covered bridge, just a third of a mile off-road, and is well worth visiting.

The Charleton Bridge was built in 1869 to carry the Charleton Road over a span of the Ashuelot River. The bridge design is a classic one span lattice truss with a length of 69 feet. The builder is unknown, but we will come to see and know a bit more about other covered bridges in our travels through New Hampshire and Vermont.

Continue on Rt. 32N another 4.5 miles to the intersection of Rt. 12. Take Rt. 12N into the city of Keene, New Hampshire.

The Charleton Covered Bridge (1869). (*Photo by the author*)

11

SCENIC BY-WAY:

ROUTE 30/100 TOWNSEND TO WESTON, VERMONT

Need a reason to travel to Townsend State Park? How about a swimming hole with a covered bridge above it within walking distance, or a stone arch that once carried the original roadway, a moderate hiking trail up a small mountain with great overlooks on Monadnock and the Green Mountains, or a charming stone house, picnic pavilion, and fireplace built for the park office and facilities during the depression era by the Civilian Conservation Corps.

The C.C.C. was a volunteer public relief corps from 1933–1942, and a number of state parks throughout New England, and indeed the country, received new roads, bridges, trail systems, and updated facilities through their efforts. Some 3 million men served in the C.C.C. during the Great Depression. It provided men work, pay, shelter, and three meals a day as they worked on projects.

Here at the park, they felled trees, constructed roads, and cut the gradual trail up Bald Mountain. They also built a nature center to educate the public, and constructed the wooden camping platforms that still occupy some sites today.

Townsend State Park has the distinction of being the first parcel in Vermont purchased for the purpose of a state park in 1912. It was then the Townsend State Forest and had been secured through the interest of Howard R. Rice and the West River Valley Association. As the state used the land for timber management, a fire tower was erected on the top of Bald Mountain in 1924. By 1927, the forest had nearly 1,000 campers during the season. The C.C.C. were encamped here during the 1933–38 seasons, working on the park improvements and constructing a new access road to Bald Mountain.

Today, the park holds some thirty tent or trailer sites as well as four lean-to sites. My brother, Bill, and I camped out for a few days her in the summer of 2019. Among the first things we did at the park was to climb Bald Mountain.

The trail leads from the road beside the stone facilities and wands through the camping area to a wooden bridge that crosses "Negro Brook," and ascends along the brook for some distance. The trail climbs and moderates with regularity, Negro Brook continues on to the West River on the opposite side of State Park Road. The switchbacks on the trail take the hiker for long lengths of walking through leveled pathways in the forest, before ascending for shorter lengths to a different level and back again. The summit is reached for the average hiker in little more than an hour, with fine views to the east of Monadnock and to the west of the Green Mountains.

If you would like a shorter, easier hike, continue past the park entrance for a quarter of a mile to the swimming hole at the West River and the Scott Covered Bridge.

Turn left, leaving the park entrance, and continue on what is now Stone Arch Road. Shortly after leaving the park entrance, look left and you will notice a finely crafted stone arch bridge, which carried the original State Forest Road over Negro Brook.

The bridge is the work of James Otis Follet, a local farmer. Follet served as a road commissioner, and through his experiences with that office and self-education, he became a home-skilled mason. Follet would build some forty stone arch bridges in Townsend and surrounding communities between 1894 and his death in 1911.

The Negro Brook Bridge spans 14.5 feet across the brook, with a height of 5 feet. A nearby bridge constructed by Follet over Fair Brook has a span of 22 feet and rests on abutments that are part stone and part bedrock, suggesting an earlier bridge had once been there.

In 1976, the Follet Stone Arch Bridge district was listed on the National Register of Historic Places, encompassing that part of southwest Townsend that holds four of Follet's stone arch bridges. The surrounding area once held seven such bridges, but three have been lost to floods or human destruction.

I never discovered the origin of the brook's name, and while the bridge retains the name, and it is still named as such in a number of books and articles, more modern maps seem to have removed the name entirely.

Continue walking, and in short time you will notice the length of Scott Bridge as it stretches over the West River. When you reach the bridge itself, you will be awed at its length and its construction. This bridge was once the primary conduit from the road across West River, a drive my brother and I considered to be now some 3–4 miles to reach the same point today, without the use of the bridge.

Scott Bridge was constructed in 1870 by Harrison Chamberlain, and at 227 feet, it is the second-longest covered bridge in the state. Its construction required three different kinds of support, with a town lattice truss that spans 166 feet, two kingspost trusses with a combined length of 111 feet, and

Stone arch bridge built by James Otis Follet (*c.* 1894). This bridge carried the original forest road to Bald Mountain. (*Photo by the author*)

Scotts Bridge (1870), the second longest covered span in Vermont. (*Photo by the author*)

laminated arches to support the town lattice. The bridge has a width of 20 feet, with a roadway of 16 feet to serve as a one-lane conveyance for travelers. The sides and gable ends have vertical wood siding.

The bridge was placed on the National Register in 1973, and has been modified three times to improve the structure. During the most recent modification, in an attempt to bring a more authentic model to the original addition, the builders removed a long-standing platform along the upstream side of the river, long used by local kids to leap from into a 10-foot-deep pool below.

In placing on new siding, they constructed small, triangular windows, as had the original to light the interior of the bridge. With the platform gone, a local man told me the kids have begun squeezing through the windows and leaping from there. For a less risky swim, a path beside the bridge leads to a sandbank and watering hole.

You may see other "swimming holes" along the embankment as you return to the park. Please be mindful of the neighbor's private property and only swim by the bridge as designated for park visitors. Take any trash back with you to the park and the dumpsters there.

To proceed with our journey, leave Townsend Park and follow State Park Road out to Rt. 30N. Take a left and proceed towards the center of Townsend. A late nineteenth-century description of the town reads:

> Townsend is a little post village in the southern part of the town, lying in a valley that is girted about by abrupt and rocky hills, one of which, Peaked mountain, rising from the east, attains an altitude of 750 feet above the village common. This common, or park, lies in the center of the village, being occupied by the Congregational Church. It was leased to the town in 1803 "for as long as the town shall maintain the church which stands theron." At that time it was such a rough, rocky piece of wild land that "an oxcart could not be drawn across it without being capsized." It is now, however, a beautiful level green, shaded by handsome maples

Today, little has changed on the main green, bordered by the intersections of Rt. 30 and Rt. 35. The shops of tinsmiths, blacksmiths, and millinary shops are gone, replaced by a pizza parlor, a modern brick town hall, and an antique store advertising "Barn Sale."

Bear left as you enter the center of town to remain on Rt. 30N. Glimpses of the West River appear on your left, and in a short time, you will notice the famed Scott Bridge as it reaches the northern bank of the river. The bridge was closed to traffic in 2012 after it was found to be structurally unsound for motorists.

Just ahead is Townsend Lake, a riverine reservoir formed from the construction of Townsend Dam. The earthen dam built in 1961 by the Army

Corps of Engineers and has a height of 126 feet and a length of 1,700 feet at its crest. As with the region around which Tully Dam was built, the area of Townsend was repeatedly flooded, the entire village of Harmonyville was washed out in the 1922 flood. The dam impounds the West River for flood control and seasonal storm water management.

You can walk or drive across the steel grated bridge on Dam Road and glance down far below to the earthworks and the river spilling out to hasten upstream. At the end of the long parking lot for the dam is a hand-painted sign on a guardrail that points you to a thin sliver of trail that leads down the bank to the West River Trail. This short extension of the larger trail follows the river from this point just west of the highway until it crosses the Tannery Brook and heads north-east to reach Rt. 30 just behind the Townsend Dam Diner.

Journeying along the route by car, you may want to stop at the general store amid the grouping of houses and buildings just past the diner. At the edge of the large parking lot are two historical markers in memory of Clarina Howard Nichols. Mrs. Nichols was born into a prosperous West Townsend family in 1810. After a disastrous first marriage, she was left destitute and supported her children by writing for the *Windham County Gazette*, a newspaper in Brattleboro, Vermont.

She married the paper's publisher and editor George Nichols and took over his duties when he became invalid. Through her work with the newspaper, Mrs. Nichols promoted many of the issues addressed by reform movements of the time including women's rights, temperance, and slavery.

Clarina also helped with organizing woman's rights activities in the east, while writing petitions to the Vermont legislature in 1852 to give women the right to vote in school meetings.

Mrs. Nichols and her family would later move to Quindaro, Kansas, to fight the expansion of slavery into that state. While there, she was active as an Underground Railroad Station Master and Conducter. She also wrote, lectured, and obtained a law degree to further her activism. She died still active in these causes in California at the age of seventy-four.

Reaching Jamaica, bear close attention as Rt. 100S bears left and Rt. 30/100N continues straight past a large garage and smattering or rural houses, sheds, and barns. Passing the intersection of a small lane that veered gently off to the right called Turkey Mountain Road, my brother and I wondered aloud how many Turkey Mountains there were in New England. Despite my expectations, when I got home and researched the question, it turns out there is only one. The road also follows Turkey Mountain Brook. You can visit pretty Hamilton Falls nearby to the east.

Suddenly on the right is a large colonial farm appears: the Georgian five-bay window over-four house with a Federal doorway, an extended pavilion to an open carriage barn to the left of the house, with a long barn extending from the right towards the open fields. A rusting tin roof capped the weathered house and barn, and a long, whitewashed chicken coop sits on a trailer at the edge of the extended half-circle drive that curved before the whole estate.

Rt. 30/100N continues along the border of the Winhall Municipal Forest for the next 7–8 miles. Glimpses of Stratton Mountain and the surrounding foothills may be seen to the west, while to the east, gently rolling hills undulate above the treeline as you drive past.

The road crosses the West River once again, and glimpses of it appear on the right as you make your way to the center of the village of Jamaica. Soon after the sign for the village, a large cemetery appears on the right and a few intermittent houses as you approach the town beneath the shadow of Ball Mountain.

Named for the Natick indigenous people's word for "beaver" rather than the Caribbean island, the first settlements were in East Jamaica before road improvements shifted the focus to what is the center of the village now. As you enter the center, a small brick library that was originally one of fourteen one-room schoolhouses in the district. Then appears and then the handsome colonial Three Mountain Inn (*c.* 1780).

The inn offers seventeen luxuriously furnished rooms within its colonial setting, and has its own pub and award-winning restaurant. The town hall appears on the left, constructed as a Universalist meetinghouse in 1851, the structure was meant to mimic the large Jamaica Community Church on the right, which was built in 1808. Services were held in the Universalist church for only a few years. By 1875, the Jamaican Drama Club had taken over the building, and renamed it as the town Opera House. They constructed a rear wing and the entryway that remains today as a vestibule with a ticket window. The club sold the building to the town in 1921, and since then it has been used for town meetings, plays, concerts, and the occasional wedding. In 2005, a three-year restoration project began, and was completed in time for the town meeting in 2008.

Further down, an old-fashioned general store offers gods of all variety. The first store in town was the Noon House, built in 1803.

Across the street, at the intersection of Pike's Falls Road, lies the old Jamaica Inn (1814) constructed as the popularity of traveling along the improved road began to grow. Known as Jamaica House when it opened its doors, it became a popular stop for travelers carried by coach between Manchester and Brattleboro.

As the village lies at the confluence of West River and Ball Mountain brook, numerous dams for industry were built, and by the early nineteenth century, when Merino sheep were imported to graze on the hillsides, Jamaica was a prosperous wool-manufacturing community.

General store in Jamaica, Vermont. (*Photo by the author*)

All of that changed, of course, with the coming of the Civil War and the decline in the market for wool. The lands that had been cleared for flocks of sheep became forest again, and the railroad soon replaced the traffic on the once well-traveled road. As you travel the existing road, remnants of those stagecoach days remain in the low-slung colonial homes along the road, and especially the grand Victorian house that borders the edge of the historic district, before the bridge leading out of the village center.

The village of Jamaica and other West River Valley towns attempted to bring the railroad through their villages on a spur they chartered as the West River Railroad, which would run from Brattleboro, Vermont to Whitehall, New York. Though the W.R.R. had been granted a charter in 1867, the proposal languished for a decade before work even began on the first segment of the line, leaving Brattleboro for Londonderry.

The railroad was never extended beyond the Londonderry depot. As you continue along Rt. 30/100N, you will reach the village of South Londonderry, where an old depot from the West River Railroad lies near the intersection of Rt. 30/100. Watch for the Londonderry Inn on the left as the road curves downhill and towards the bridge across the West River and the intersection just beyond. Take a sharp right to park near the depot, or continue straight through the intersection and park at the Corner Market and Deli just ahead, at the intersection of Middle Road and Main Street.

This classic country store was built in 1868 and early on became L. H. Lanman's Hardware Store. The proprietor had run a long-established store across the intersection for some years, but with the loss of that

Depot in south Londonderry, Vermont. Note the distance to St. Johnsbury on the sign. (*Photo by the author*)

Originally a hardware store, the Corner Market and café now does a brisk business at the crossroads of Rt. 100. (*Photo by the author*)

building to fire, he purchased the store and established business at this location.

The large three-story building, with a 7,000-square-foot barn attached above and below ground, was used for multiple purposes. The third floor held a popular dance hall, and a boxing club set up a gymnasium and ring in the spacious basement. For the past fifteen years, the old building has largely contained a general store and café type of business. The store's latest owner, Jason O'Connor, appreciates the history of the building and has incorporated old shipping boxes, tools, and memorabilia from the store's hardware days into the displays for goods around the store.

While still serving as a grocery store, the main draw to the Corner Store is the deli and soup and sandwich offerings of the café' inside. As I talked with Jason about his hopes for continued success with the store, I devoured a lobster bisque and roast beef sandwich.

Rt. 100N continues on past the intersection, turning left as you cross the bridge, or a right turn out of the Corner Market parking lot past Middle Road. The route becomes a country road again, slipping past low-slung wide-hipped roof houses, a reminder that you are in snow country once the winter arrives. Woodlands interspersed by rural dwellings pass by, the spectacular red multi-storied barn of the Anjali Farm comes into view on the right, with the farmstand tucked back from the roadside. The barn itself now houses the West River Montessori School.

Not far down the road, you will see a wooden sign for Grandma Millers Pies and Pastries that sits on the edge of the lawn of a large nineteenth-century farmhouse, with a large barn beyond that serves as the production center for the business.

Grandma Miller's Pies and Pastries are named for Dorothy Miller, the owners' grandmother who baked pies on a family owned farm in Iowa. Her baking skills were passed along to her daughter, Betty Miller Nunnikkhoven, who began a business in Connecticut. Her son, David, was soon baking as well, and after graduating from the International School for the Pastry Arts in Elmsford, New York, he began baking and supplying pies to several local stores.

He opened the barn and adjacent café in 2001. The bakery offers seventeen varieties of pie, including the traditional apple pies, blackberry-peach, burgundy pie (blueberries and cranberries), and black bottom bourbon pecan. They also offer specialty pastries and frozen entrees to bring home. I may well make a return trip for pies as Thanksgiving approaches.

The route continues along, following the West River until reaching Londonderry and the intersection of Rt. 11. The routes merge as you enter the village. Bear right at the intersection past a shopping mall, and continue on Rt. 11/100 past the liquor store and a diner, then look for Rt. 100N to bear left just past an ancient house on the right, and another low-slung building advertised as the "Shoe Barn".

An ancient house just before the continuation of Rt. 100. (*Photo by the author*)

Take Rt. 100N uphill through another grouping of old homes. Bear left as you pass Pond Street and continue past the Phoenix Fire Company station on the right. Resuming a drive through farmland and forested areas, the road curves to the right at the intersection of Johnson Hill Road, and crosses the west River again, before continuing past Boynton Road.

Farther along, you will spot a weathered barn on the left, and an expansive colonial house and extended buildings on the right. This is the Colonial House Inn. The original dwelling is said to have been built between 1790 and 1810 as the Richardson Farm. The family lived on the property until the mid-1960s, and in 1967, the house and 12 acres were sold to Jean and Chuck savage who renovated the house to provide rooms for an inn and renovated a living room for guests. The following year, they added motel rooms 1–7 by purchasing the historic Palmer house in Manchester, Vermont, and cutting it into sections, and carting it across the mountains to be repurposed here. A dining room and two more motel suites were added in 1974 before the inn was sold in 1979 to Betty and John Nunnikhoven.

The couple ran the motel for the next twenty-three years, raising their children in the motel; a daughter and son-in-law operate the establishment today. It remains a unique roadside attraction, and no doubt a destination for generations of visitors.

Rt. 100N continues on past acres of cultivated fields before bearing left at the intersection of Foster Road before entering the center of the village of Weston.

The village is the home of the Vermont Country Store, and as that has been an attraction since opening in 1949, this and other Main Street attractions

The Vermont Country Store, a fixture in town since 1949. (*Photo by the author*)

usually leave parking at a minimum. As the Colonial Inn at Weston and the clock on the towered white belfry of the Weston Church comes into view, you have reached the center of the village. Continue past the famed store on the right and the village store a little further down on the opposite side of Main Street, and take a left at Lawrence Hill Road to find parking around the common and explore the town. A large parking lot is also available just past the end of the common off Main Street next to the Historical Society.

Weston has so much more to offer beyond the country store destination, and the community has worked very hard along with their historically minded inhabitants to preserve the original community, and make it part of the attraction for visitors. The common itself is an unusually large green space to have survived this long, unscathed, uncut, and undiminished as in so many other New England towns. The reason lies in the story behind the green itself, for rather than being a survivor from colonial times, today's green was a frog pond owned by one Oliver Farrar who lived in the white, Federal mansion house just past the end of the common, which is now home to the Weston Historical Society.

In 1886, a group of nine ladies in the community formed a committee with the intent of "establishing and maintaining a public park in the town of Weston." Farrar parted with the pond, it was duly filled in, and the Farrar

Park Association was formed and chartered by the Vermont General assembly, with the land deeded out to the nine ladies of the Association.

The park remains maintained under the trustees of the association. With its classic white gazebo, and proximity to the Greek temple-like entry to the Weston Playhouse, it is a popular gathering place for festivals and events.

Beyond the Farrar-Mansur House is the old town well, and a mill with a large waterwheel built on the site where a 1790 sawmill had once stood. The mill is also a craftsman's center and museum that exhibits a collection of early tools and machinery, a tinsmith peddler's wagon, and, in the fire museum, a Concord Coach.

The day of my visit, I met David Claggett, a tinsmith who had been at the Old Mill Museum for over twenty years. He was cleaning out his shop, retiring after years of working and making early American reproductions for Williamsburg, Old Sturbridge Village, and other places. He showed me the wagon he had purchased and restored, a typical peddler's wagon from the 1880s, capable of storing a variety of wares in its many cupboards and drawers built within the wagon.

The compound around the museum also includes a small barn-like structure that served in the early 1900s as the town firehouse. In 1936, the Vermont Guild of old-time crafts established a working museum on the site as it remains today.

True craftsmen like David Claggett are a diminishing figure in the world of re-enactment and colonial museums. For a colonial craftsman today, whether they be a tinsmith, blacksmith, cobbler, harness maker, or soap and candle-maker, a store, even in the midst of a colonial museum, cannot sustain the work alone. That means traveling to fairs and festivals every weekend through the season, and hoping you make enough to create enough product for the following year. It is a grueling life, though seldom have I heard people in the re-enactment and museum communities complain. Their love of history and imparting it to others sustains them, as it has every historian who has set out to write a story of a particular place and time.

Walking south past the Historical Society and the Weston Playhouse, look for the bridge that crosses the West River and carries Lawrence Hill Road. It offers a fine view of the river, and of the well-preserved colonial inn called Riverview.

The small Wilder Memorial Library can be found just past the inn as Lawrence Hill climbs the hill to reach Trout Club Road and Wantastiquet Lake. Walking back to Main Street, past the new post office, visit the general store to replenish supplies for the road, have an ice cream at the adjacent stand, and then prepare to visit the iconic Vermont Country Store.

A place of distant wonder to me as a child, I would pore through the old almanac-like catalogs on my grandmother's sofa and picture a store with a

The large waterwheel and Craftsman's Museum at the site of a 1790 sawmill. (*Photo by the author*)

Riverview Inn lies adjacent to the river, across from the town green. (*Photo by the author*)

long oak counter, a pot-bellied woodstove at its center, and shelves filled with the cornucopia of gadgets, clothing, winter gear, camping cookware, wool blankets, and foodstuffs of all kinds—from smoked meats to jams and jellies, and, of course, maple syrup.

The Vermont country store is, of course, all that and more, though I was disappointed on my visit not to find a classic cast-iron waffling pan. The store has an abundance of handmade toys for children, as well as a bakery and café to take a breather while waiting for others to finish shopping.

Take your time returning to your car after visiting Main Street and walk back along the common. If you are fortunate as I was that afternoon, you may hear a rehearsal from the playhouse as the music wafts across the shaded green.

12

OVER THE RIVER AND THROUGH THE WOODS:

ROUTE 121 BELLOWS FALLS TO NORTH WINDHAM, VERMONT

Like Tully Dam, the town of Bellows Falls was an iconic stop on our family vacations. Cross the bridge over the Connecticut River, and you literally drive from New Hampshire into Vermont. A bridge has been at this crossing since colonial times, and by the nineteenth century, it had become part of the Green Mountain turnpike.

The village was settled near the falls that the indigenous Abenaki people had once used for fishing shad and salmon as they spurned upriver. The English settlers who arrived in 1753 called it Great Falls, and later changed the town name after a landowner named Col. Benjamin Bellows.

Col. Enoch Hale constructed the first bridge across the river in 1785. It remained the only bridge over the river until another bridge was built at Springfield in 1796. The original bridge was replaced several times. The original Bellows Falls Arch Bridge over which my family crossed was constructed in 1905, and it was the longest spanning arch bridge in the United States at that time. It was replaced with a new arch bridge in 1982, another bridge downriver called the Charles N. Vilas Bridge was built in 1930 and was closed to all but pedestrian traffic in 2009.

The site also has the distinction of being the first town where a canal was constructed by a British-based company between 1791 and 1802. When completed, the canal was 22 feet wide with a depth of 4 feet. It held nine locks that were each 75 feet long and 20 feet wide, allowing ships to pass around the falls by lifting them 52 feet around the gorge.

The railroad came to Bellows Falls in 1849 and while greatly reducing the river traffic, precipitated the rise of mill industries in town, which then used the canal almost exclusively for water power. By 1875, the canal was enlarged

Railroad bridge across the Connecticut River in Bellows Falls, Vermont. (*Photo by the author*)

to a width of 75 feet, with a depth of 17 feet; at the turn of the century, it was supplying power to numerous paper and textile mills in the village.

The wealth of the mills allowed many of the fine civic buildings and Victorian houses in the village to be built during the nineteenth century. In fact, the village neighborhood historic district holds the largest concentration of well-preserved nineteenth-century dwellings in southern Vermont.

As kids, the place we liked in Bellows Falls the most was the Miss Bellows Falls Diner. We always entered town and parked in the lot adjacent to the dining car. We kids could have a coke while our dad drank coffee, and I recall having my first piece of apple pie *à la mode* with him in the diner. If my memory recalls, he added maple syrup to his ice cream over the pie. Our father was a man of hard work and few pleasures that he afforded himself. This was one he allowed himself for as long as I can remember.

Today, Bellows Falls is more accessible to the traveler, with Amtrak service at the old train station. The town seems to have added a number of shops and restaurants that give jobs to the locals. The pleasant woman cooking breakfast at the diner had worked in Manhattan for many years before transplanting herself here with her husband, who had family nearby. She lived on the New Hampshire side of the river and had a few neighbors within several miles. The quiet and early closings took some getting used to, but she bore it out, even after her husband's passing, and made a home for herself here. She travels back to New York to see her daughter and enjoy foods that are not on the local menus. Amtrak service has made that easier, she told me. No more white-knuckle drives on the highway.

The diner was constructed in 1922 by the Worcester Lunch Car Company as No. 771 and has sat on Rochester Street since the mid-1940s. The barrel-roofed metal structure, measuring 18 by 31 feet, lies parallel to the road. It was originally built for Frank Willie and John Korsak for their "Frankie and Johnny's Diner" in Lowell, Massachusetts. When the men were recruited for World War II, they sold the diner to an investor in Bellows Falls, where it replaced an earlier diner at this location. Today, it is believed to be that only surviving barrel-roofed "Worcester diner" in the state. It has been listed on the National Register of Historic Places since 1983.

Take some time to explore the downtown area with its more modern shops and restaurants built in the shadows of the grand civic buildings of the nineteenth century, the church-like Rockingham town hall where the Opera House is now located, the square that has been the hub of the city since first settled, and the old train station on Depot Street.

The downtown area suffered a serious fire in 1921 that destroyed many of the buildings, including the original train station that had been built in 1851. The present station was constructed on the site in 1922–23. It was closed when passenger service ended to Bellows Falls in 1966.

Revival came in 1972, when Amtrak reopened the line with resumption of the Washington, D.C.–Montreal route that earlier trains had taken. Passengers

Miss Bellows Falls Diner (1922), Bellows Falls, Vermont. (*Photo by the author*)

were carried aboard the *Montrealer* for most of the years between 1972 and 1995. Since then, a train called the *Vermonter* runs the route daily.

Continue west along the main drag. You will see an old-fashioned general store straight ahead, across the intersection of Rt. 5. Continue straight and enter the beginning of one of the oldest and most scenic drives in Vermont. Rt. 121 crosses the Saxton's River four times in the next 8 miles. Keep an eye out as you see the road and the river come closely together, small side lots created for fly fishermen can be seen during these stretches of the road.

One of the first buildings you will notice heading out of Bellows Falls is the massive S. L. Moore building on the left. A cluster of houses passes and you quickly enter the village of North Westminster, originally called Gageville and grown as a community around the Gage Basket Factory built along the Saxtons River, after first establishing itself on Morse Brook in 1842. The factory produced baskets for farm and household use from local wood. It remained in business until the 1940s when it was destroyed by fire.

Many of the houses along this stretch of Rt. 121 were homes of the factory workers. The community also expanded at the turn of the twentieth century and with the construction of a trolley line between the villages of Saxton's River and Bellows Falls.

In the mid-nineteenth century, prize merino sheep were imported to fill the village pastures, each farmer selling the wool at a competitive price to one of the many wool mills that developed along the Saxton's River.

A tannery, paper mill, sawmills, and a box factory have all at one time or another been constructed downstream of the rocky gorge that spills Twin Falls through the community. With such production, comes the need for more efficient transportation of goods. In those days, wooden bridges were in constant need of repair or replacement, often wiped out during spring floods. In time, more advanced construction brought sturdier bridges erected on stone embankments and raised up so that carriages initially went uphill to enter them.

One such bridge can be seen on the right shortly after Barber's Park Road. The Hall Bridge was one of seventeen covered bridges that once existed in the town of Rockingham. Built by Sanford Granger, a prominent bridge builder in Windham County, it is dated between 1867 and 1871. When the town applied for the bridge to be placed on the National Register of Historic Places in 1973, the description of the bridge read:

> The Hall Covered Bridge consists of a single span, supported by twin Town Lattice trusses. At each corner of the bridge, an iron buttress extends from an extended floor beam to the upper side of the bridge, providing lateral support for its superstructure ... the abutments are constructed of stone slabs without mortar. The bridge is 117 feet long and fifteen feet wide, with a 12-foot roadway.

The Hall Covered
Bridge (1871)
reconstructed in 1982.
(*Photo by the author*)

The description continued:

> On the exterior, the large planks pegged together diagonally to form the trusses
> (and side walls) of the bridge are sheathed with flush boards hung vertically.
> Similar siding protects the ends of the trusses immediately inside the portals.
> There are three small diamond shaped windows in the west side of the bridge
> and small diamond shaped openings (one irregular) in the east side. The gable
> ends are sheathed with flush boards hung horizontally. The roof of the bridge is
> covered with corrugated metal sheeting

By that period, the condition of the original bridge, as described, was becoming
precarious. Guy cables were installed from the bridge to the riverbanks to
provide additional support, but in 1980, an overweight truck attempting to
cross the bridge brought about its destruction. The bridge you see today is a
replica of the original built in 1982 by Milton S. Graton who recreated the
bridge to the last hand-hewn detail and had a team of oxen haul it into place.

The bridge is but 1.2 miles east of Saxton's River Village, and as you approach the modern bridge festooned with flower boxes and flags, you may appreciate how modern engineering has made such passages routine and without incident.

A stone house attached to a large wooden barn is on the left as you approach the bridge, and just a little further down the road you will enter Saxton's River Village. The village was settled in 1783. A meetinghouse was built shortly thereafter, and a cemetery established in 1810. A textile mill was constructed as early as 1815 at Middle Falls, now called Saxton's River Falls.

Saxton's Falls Village was connected with Bellows Falls, as mentioned earlier, by Railroad between 1900 and 1924. The train was run on an electrical system powered by the stations at Great Falls in the latter village. Crossing the bridge and passing Oak Street on the right, you see a large, high-dormered meetinghouse, a large farmhouse, and, across the lane, a large three building complex comprised of a barn, an extension, and house, which carries you toward another assortment of buildings and a lengthy twelve-bay tenement with a porch that runs the length of the bottom three-quarters of the building. The lot on which it sits extends to Mill Road where the west side of the structure holds another ten windows. This massive building was likely a nineteenth-century tenement for mill workers during the height of village industry. The tannery, textile mills, and distillery in the village had all disappeared by the 1920s.

The white spire and clapboarded frame of the First Congregational Church (1836) comes into view on the left as you enter the village center. Across the street lies the red-clapboarded Saxton's River Village Market (1870), first operated as Simmonds store.

The village also holds the Saxton's River Inn (1803), a Baptist church built in 1840, and the Main Street Arts, a non-profit institute that provides musicals, community events, educational classes, and gallery shows to the local community. They are housed in a former Hardware store (1830) that, along with the small white schoolhouse on the corner of Main and School Street and the many of the other buildings in the village, is part of the historical district listed on the National Register.

Leaving the village, bear right at the Baptist Church and the small rotary that forms the intersection of Main Street and Westminster Street. Another old mill appears on the left—its distinctive doorway at the end of the original building, before the addition of a small house. Just beyond, a large dirt lot opens up adjacent to the water, and a large dirt lot accommodates boaters and fishermen as a put in along the river.

A group of rural houses pass and then an attractive Victorian inn on a hillside draws your attention to the right; this is Moore's Guest House. Continue along, and the road again becomes a country lane. Bear left at the intersection of Pleasant Valley Road and continue past acres of farmland and

Saxton's River Village Market (1870). (*Photo by the author*)

cultivated fields to the south, while woodlands dominate the northern side of the road. Assorted businesses, trailers, and houses appear intermittently in the otherwise unchanging landscape.

The river comes close again for a stretch, past Leach Road, though I saw no easy access along the road. A green strip of land ahead provides a barrier for the traffic slowing for a turn on to the one-lane steel and concrete bridge that crosses the river at McBride Road on the left. Continue along Rt. 121W for several more miles and you will reach the village of Cambridgeport.

A large farm appears as you reach the outskirts, and then a grouping of houses. A small parking space appears on the left beside an exposed portion of the river before a sluice carries it beneath the bridge at the crossing.

At the bridge over Weaver Brook, just past the intersection of Cambridgeport Road on the right, you will notice the ruins of an old stone mill. As local historian Ken Aiken described, this was one of the many woolen mills in the area built in 1836. It was destroyed in one of the disastrous fires that would visit the town through the nineteenth and into the early twentieth century.

The center of the village was destroyed by fire in 1930. Damages from floods also ravaged the village in 1927, and again in 1936 and 1937, followed by the hurricane of 1938.

Continuing on, you will come to another bridge at the entrance to Grafton. Just before the bridge is a stone house that functioned as part of a soapstone mill to finish the stone quarried on nearby Kidder Hill, which was at one time the second largest soapstone quarry in the United States.

Serpentine stone was dragged from the quarry to the river on sleds pulled by oxen. The mill at the site also produced heating stones, griddles, and inkwells

Ruins of an old woolen mill, at the corner of Cambridgeport Road and Rt. 121. (*Photo by the author*)

for household use. Between here and the center of Grafton were six dams that once supported a woolen mill, a gristmill, and the soapstone mill at this location.

The center of Grafton is 4 miles from the intersection. Take a right and continue on Rt. 121. The village of Grafton is, in my humble opinion, one of the prettiest towns in the state of Vermont. As a writer, researcher, and long walker, there is much to appreciate about the town. You will know you are at the village center when the old fire station and post office appear on the right.

The cottage-like post office and the two-story garage-like fire station with its high piedmont roof are a proper introduction to a village that is one of the most civic minded, and historically preserved villages in Windham County.

Across the street from the post office lies the town library, which occupies an elegant early nineteenth-century house known as the Butterfield House, a two and a half-story wood-frame house with a gable roof, a granite foundation, and five-over four-bay windows and a federal doorway facing Main Street, though its main entrance is at the eastern façade of the house that, as an extension, supports a two-storied portico with supporting polygonal columns beneath the pedimented attic story of the house. An older one and a half-story ell on the south end of the existing house is believed to have been the original structure on the site, which was purchased by John Butterfield in 1811.

Post office, Grafton, Vermont. (*Photo by the author*)

The house as it looks today has been its appearance since the late 1860s. Its blend of Italianite and Greek Revival is actually quite common in Vermont houses built during this period. The library has occupied the house since the 1950s.

A one-time hostelry, known as the Eagle Hotel, is just a few steps away on the right-hand side of the road. Originally built as a Georgian-Federal-style house in 1826 by Lucius Alexander, the owner operated a fulling mill on the Saxton's River. He later sold his shares in the mill to Peter Alexander, and in 1831, the new owner built a similar brick house next door. This house burned down in 1839, and Alexander sold the surviving house to one Peter Davis.

The building was improved in 1840 with the addition of a Greek Revival portico with four columns supporting an arched dormer and second-story porch with wooden railing that runs the length of the façade. It became the Eagle Hotel and was the village "temperance tavern" in the days when informed scientists and doctors, as well as preachers and roving firebrands warned the public against the ravages of drinking.

The house was later the private residence of the Hall family. Fannie Hall, the family matriarch, was the village postmaster for seventy years. She was

The Eagle Hotel (1826, 1840) was the temperance tavern in the village. (*Photo by the author*)

well known to fly out of the small post office after a passing resident with mail for them in her hands. So respected was she by the town that her home became known as the Fannie Hall house, and the name of the old hotel faded from recent memory.

Today, the house is owned by Nelson Cooley, who is restoring the former elegance to what is now called Eaglebrook. He and his sister, Sandy, were waiting for the library sale to open across the street on the day of my visit. We chatted about the house and town, and they graciously gave me a bit more of the history beyond what was on a town placard.

The house will be a private residence once more, as it was originally built to be, though with a touch of elegance from its days as a hotel. It will likely have a placard placed nearby to tell its history. There are several such placards tastefully displayed throughout the village. One tells the story of Alec Turner, who settled as a free black man in town in 1873.

Turner and his wife had been born into slavery, and each found their freedom during the turbulent times of the Civil War. Alec escaped to enlist in the Union Army, while his wife, Sally, was freed at the close of the war. When the couple came to Grafton, they began to tell their story at public gatherings.

Owner Nelson Cooley and his sister, Sandy, on the porch of Eaglebrook. (*Photo by the author*)

They told of Alec's father's survival of the Middle Passage, sang "slave-songs," and led the crowds in anti-slavery ballads.

Many may have thought that the end of slavery brought about black rights, voting, and representation in one fell swoop of reunification, but that was far from the case. Freed blacks had to argue and speak out publicly like the Turners, take communities to court, and petition Congress for the freedoms that would eventually usher in a brief, but hopeful period of Reconstruction. The Turners' daughter, Daisy, would later become a well-known activist for civil rights during her own lifetime.

The Turners performed at the famed Phelps Hotel (1801), which was then the social center of the village for citizens and travelers alike. The building was originally constructed as a tavern and improved to a first-class hotel by mid-century when the village was a stagecoach hub for those line traveling across the Green Mountains to Albany. The Turners' performance raised money for the Baptist Church. The hotel is now the Grafton Inn, and it features a host of well-preserved, antique furnished rooms for visitors, as well as a five-star restaurant in the tavern.

The Phelps Barn just up the street has been turned into a tavern as well, and it is a popular place with locals to have a burger and beer. The Grafton Historical Society occupies a small house on Main Street just beyond the inn. It has a fine collection of artifacts from the village, many of which are cataloged in photographs online—a good source of reference for identifying similarities in artifacts and ephemera. The historical society was established in 1962 with a mission to "keep alive the memory of those sturdy men and women who turned a wilderness into a heritage of which the people of Grafton are proud..." as wrote historian Helen B. Pettengill (1878–1945), a native of Grafton, graduate of Mount Holyoke College, and a teacher for many years at Howard Street school and Forest Park Junior High. She never married and would live for many years on State Street, often sharing her home with her sister, Fannie, who was also unmarried.

The Grafton Historical Society's *A History of Grafton 1745–1971 and Sidelights of Grafton History* contain many of Ms. Pettengill's sketches about the local history. There is another connection to this dedicated teacher in town, which we will visit shortly.

The society would publish several author titles as well as collaborative books on the village history over the years, and the effort to preserve the Turner family homestead on Turner Hill has been an ongoing project for several years. The society maintains the museum on Main Street and the old law office situated behind the building, which is now the Turner Hill Interpretive Center. They are also responsible for the placards telling of the family's history throughout town.

The village store, which began as the John Barrett Store in 1816, is the subject of a published inventory of the store's accounts between 1816 and 1830. Barrett's account shows some 322 customers from the surrounding communities.

Spend some time in Grafton walking the side streets and visiting other sites of interest. A short walk up Townsend Street to Pleasant Street brings you to the Vermont Museum of Minerals, just further up on Townsend Street is a nature museum, and a little further beyond, as the road becomes Grafton Road, is the elegant colonial house that holds the Windham Foundation.

The Windham Foundation was established by Dean Mathey in 1963. A successful financier in New York City, Mathey spent summers here in Grafton with his cousin Matt Hall. The foundation was established to be operational, first restoring and revitalizing the Old Grafton Inn, and later the Grafton Village Cheese Company, which was reopened in 1967 with the hope of supporting the regions dairy farmers. The foundation also protects some 1,200 acres of local forest, a good part of which is accessible by trails. They are also working with the Grafton Historical Society to preserve Birchdale Camp, the site of the Turner homestead.

Today the Windham Foundation awards grants to community endeavors that support the social, economic, and cultural vitality of Vermont's rural communities.

Grafton village store, Grafton, Vermont. (*Photo by the author*)

Other sites of historical interest include the Kidder Hill Covered Bridge, which carries Kidder Hill Road over the south branch of the Saxton's River. The bridge is a single-span Queenspost structure that measures 66 feet in length with a width of 15 feet and a roadway of 12 feet. It rests on stone abutments that have been reinforced with concrete, and lies askew of the riverbed, with its trusses forming a parallelogram 15 degrees off rectangular. The bridge is sheathed with vertical plank siding and covered with a metal roof.

The original bridge at this location was constructed around 1870, and it remained the town's last-standing nineteenth-century bridge until it had to be replaced in 1995. It is Windham County's last surviving example of a Queenspost truss bridge, and only one of a handful that was built with a skew. It was nominated to be placed on the National Register of Historic Places in 2005.

The village cemetery, located a few miles back along Rt. 121, holds the graves of many of the townsmen lost in the Civil War, a good number of them who died from casualties suffered in the Battle of Gettysburg.

To continue on Rt. 121W, leave the village by bearing right on to Houghtonville Road and the large white church on the corner. The road quickly becomes a gravel drive and continues as such past long stretches of woodland. A small bridge crosses Hinkley Brook on the right, and the road continues past acres of forest, intermittently broken by an open field, and a house and barn.

More open spaces soon appear on the sides of the road, though be mindful of tractors that may be traveling through this section of the road. A small frog puddle appears on the left in the midst of a well-manicured lawn. A pair of picnic tables are available as well as a "portajohn" in the shade of a young maple. There was no sign to indicate a park, but it clearly is maintained as one.

Continuing on Rt. 121W, you will again pass acres of agricultural fields and the farm to which they belong, with its tin-roofed farmhouse, so popular in Vermont, and brightly painted barns with cupolas that likely held weathervanes. More fenced-in fields follow, with a long rail fence running the length of the property along the road, even behind the remains of a stonewall that once bordered the fields. The property is currently used as a horse farm.

Continue past the intersection of Woden Farm Road on the left, and pass through another long stretch of wooded area as you approach the border of the Putnam State Forest. As you near the intersection with the forest road, an open space suddenly appears on the left, with a well-preserved, one-room schoolhouse.

This is the Pettengill school named after Senator Samuel B. Pettengill, who represented the third Congressional district of Indiana, but whose family had long held roots in Grafton. Born in Oregon, Pettengill's family moved back to Grafton in 1892, and lived on their ancestral farm established by his great-

The Pettengill Schoolhouse, Grafton, Vermont. (*Photo by the author*)

grandfather in 1787. He attended common schools in the village and later graduated from Middlebury College; he obtained a law degree from Yale University by 1911.

The schoolhouse was built on land given by the Pettengill family to the village, and it was one of thirteen that originally provided education for the district. It was the second schoolhouse built in Grafton in 1856. It operated as a school until 1937.

The schoolhouse was most recently owned, restored, and maintained over the last thirty years by a man who became one of the most beloved citizens of Grafton. Danny Michaelson was a faculty member of Bennington College for many years, and between creative pursuits and his long-standing involvement with community groups, he maintained the schoolhouse and shared its history. He was appointed to the board of directors of the Grafton Historical Society before his untimely death in December 2018.

Take a left to continue on Rt. 121W as the road continues as a gravel drive through a forested area until its intersection with Rt. 11. From here, take a left to go to Rt. 30 South, back to Townsend.

BIBLIOGRAPHY

ARTICLES

Clark, E., "Early Historical Highlights of the Town of Canaan," Town of Canaan website, www.webtownhall.com/canaan/Resources/History.aspx

Cranston, G. T., "A Rome Point Boxwood has Boss Connections," *The Independent*, North Kingstown, July 14, 2016

Durwin, J., "The Decline of Loyalist Opposition in the Berkshires," iBerkshires.com, July 6, 2014

Sander, P., architect, "Pomfret Street Historic District," Gombach Group, 2010

National Park Service, NRHP Application for the Hall Covered Bridge, Rockingham, Vt.

BOOKS

Aiken, K., *Touring Vermonts Scenic Roads: A Comprehensive Guide* (Downeast Books, 1999)

Benedict, Rev. W. A., & Tracy, Rev. H., *A History of the Town of Sutton 1704–1876* (Worcester: Sanford & Co., 1878)

Child, H., *Gazetteer* (1884)

Cranston, G. T., *The View from Swamptown,* Vols 1 & 2 (North Kingstown: Swamptown Press, 2014)

Geake, R. A., *Historic Rhode Island Farms* (Charleston: The History Press, 2013); *Historic Taverns of Rhode Island* (Charlestown: The History Press, 2012)

Ledyard, B., *A History of the Town of Paxton, Massachusetts* (Putnam: Davis & Co., 1889)

Miller, J. R., *Early Life in Sheffield Berkshire County, Massachusetts* (Sheffield Historical Society, 2002)

ONLINE SOURCES

www.connecticuthistory.org
www.livingplaces.com/CT/Windham_County/Pomfret_Town/Pomfret_Street_
Historic_District.html
www.nhsearchroots.com
minotmainehistoricalsociety.wordpress.com
www.hearthsidehouse.org
www.historicnewengland.org

For quick facts about towns and other resources to gather more information, I visited
Wikipedia.com